30-MINUTE COOKING FOR TWO

30-Minute COOKING FOR TWO

Healthy Dishes Without All the Fuss

TAYLOR ELLINGSON

PHOTOGRAPHY BY DARREN MUIR

ROCKRIDGE
PRESS

For general information on our other products and services or to obtain technical support, please contact our Customer Care Department within the United States at (866) 744-2665, or outside the United States at (510) 253-0500.

Rockridge Press publishes its books in a variety of electronic and print formats. Some content that appears in print may not be available in electronic books, and vice versa.

TRADEMARKS: Rockridge Press and the Rockridge Press logo are trademarks or registered trademarks of Callisto Media Inc. and/or its affiliates, in the United States and other countries, and may not be used without written permission. All other trademarks are the property of their respective owners. Rockridge Press is not associated with any product or vendor mentioned in this book.

Designer: Christopher T. Fong
Editor: Pippa White
Production Editor: Erum Khan

Photography © Darren Muir

Author photo © Marc Ellingson

Cover: Hawaiian Chicken Sliders, page 70.

ISBN: Print 978-1-64152-224-3
eBook 978-1-64152-225-0

TO MARC, MY FAVORITE REASON
TO COOK FOR TWO

CONTENTS

INTRODUCTION

Welcome to *30-Minute Cooking for Two!* And welcome to the wide world of smaller-batch cooking. Whether you're single, a newlywed, an empty nester, or just plain tired of giant portions and days of leftovers, this cookbook is for you.

My interest in cooking began in graduate school when I lived alone, in my first apartment with a full kitchen. I stuck to cooking the basics for a couple of years with a rotation of meals that I was comfortable making. Eventually, though, I became bored with the same limited flavors week after week, and decided to step outside of my comfort zone. I began experimenting, became more creative, and came up with a variety of dishes that I love and still make today—even though I am not just cooking for myself anymore.

Eventually I got married, adding another mouth to the mix. These days I have two small children, but between their early bedtimes and having only one who is eating solid food so far, I am usually still cooking just for my husband and me. In the times when all four of us do sit down for a home-cooked meal together, I give my three-year-old a small portion of what we are eating, so the recipes in this book with two or three servings are doubly great for my little family. Despite the changes in my own life, I have found small-batch cooking and baking to be continually useful, and I think you will find that, too.

Beyond portion size, the majority of people I've talked to about cooking are frustrated with the lack of time they have between getting home from work or school, and needing to have dinner

on the table. We are all busy, and it can be hard to find an hour (or longer!) to cook a nice meal. Ordering in or going out gets expensive, and is not always the healthiest option.

My hope is that *30-Minute Cooking for Two* becomes your go-to cookbook for simple and delicious recipes that are easy to follow and quick to whip up. Each of these 110 recipes makes two or three servings and takes 30 minutes or less from start to finish, and most contain eight ingredients or less (excluding olive oil, salt, and pepper). You'll find recipes for any day of the week, from a quick weekday breakfast sandwich, to indulgent weekend cinnamon rolls, to Tuesday night tacos, to a proper date-night steak. With this cookbook, you will see that cooking doesn't need to be complicated, take a long time, or have 20 ingredients to make something amazing. Cooking for two means fewer leftovers, realistic portion sizes, and less processed food.

To give you even more variety, most of these recipes have a suggested ingredient swap, so you can adapt the recipe to your liking or switch it up the second time around. And don't be afraid to come up with your own variations of these recipes. Just because a recipe includes rice doesn't mean you can't try it with quinoa or pasta instead. The bottom line is to have fun with these recipes, and to use this cookbook as a jumping-off point for having delicious, fast, and easy culinary adventures!

CHAPTER ONE

WHY TWO CAN BE TRICKY

Cooking for two can be challenging for many reasons. For one, most cookbooks are geared toward large-batch cooking and have serving sizes of 6 to 8. Leftovers can be great, but it's never fun eating the same thing for days and days on end.

Even when you scale recipes back, you are left with half-used packages of food that take up cabinet space and often end up forgotten. Use these tips to help you navigate the grocery store and organize your kitchen to decrease waste and make the most of your space at home.

SHOPPING FOR TWO

When it comes to shopping for two, meal prep and planning are key. The following tips mainly address what to buy in small portions versus large portions to stick to your budget and reduce waste.

Meat. Try to buy straight from the butcher/fishmonger as often as you can. That way you can get exactly what you need. Most prepackaged meat comes in 1-pound increments, which is often too much for two people. If you don't have the option to buy from the counter, and prepackaged meat is your only option, be sure to freeze what you don't need immediately. Place the leftover portion in a plastic bag and label with the quantity and date.

Vegetables. Buy your vegetables from a market where you can choose the quantity you need, as opposed to produce wrapped in packages. Many recipes call for small-size vegetables, so be aware of the size of vegetables that you select at the grocery store.

Grains. For items that I use often, such as rice, quinoa, and oats, I prefer to buy them in the self-serve bulk section of the store. It's usually cheaper than buying prepackaged grains, and I store any extra in my bulk bins at home. If it's an item I don't use often, such as wild rice or oat bran, buying in bulk lets me get the exact amount I need for a recipe, so there's no waste.

Canned goods. Buy canned goods as you need them. Even though they last a long time, canned goods can clutter a kitchen pantry. This makes it difficult to keep tabs on what you have on hand. I always have the canned goods that I list in my pantry staples, but beyond that, I buy them as needed.

Oil. Since olive oil is used in almost every recipe that I cook, I also buy it in bulk. It's cheaper this way and I know it will get used. I use an olive oil dispenser that I keep handy on the counter, and I store the rest in my basement kitchen-supply closet.

Dairy. Unless you're feeding a family of four or more, you really don't need to buy large quantities of dairy. Buy what you need for one week. This prevents any excess from spoiling and reduces waste. Since butter usually comes in packs of four, whatever I don't plan on using within a couple of weeks is stored in the freezer.

Dried fruit and nuts. It's more economical to buy dried fruit and nuts in bulk. They tend to last for quite a while, so the extra amount won't spoil quickly. Be sure to portion them out in mason jars or glass containers in your pantry so they're easy to spot and within reach. Store any remaining amounts in the freezer.

Frozen vegetables. Buy your frozen vegetables in whatever portion you think will work best. I go back and forth between smaller and larger bags. It all depends on how much room I have in my freezer. If you're concerned about cost and have plenty of space, frozen vegetables are fairly inexpensive, so the larger bags may be more economical.

Frozen fruit. I always buy frozen fruit in larger bags. It's by far the cheaper option. Frozen fruit is perfect for smoothies, so if you eat the way I do, you'll end up going through large amounts before you know it.

Snacks. Along with fruit and nuts, I typically buy our snacks in bulk. Items such as chips, hummus, salsa, granola bars, apples, bananas, and crackers are all staples in my household. We go through them fairly quickly, so buying in bulk seems right.

PANTRY STAPLES

Pantry staples allow you to create meals at the last minute. These are the items that you typically have in your pantry, refrigerator, and freezer at any given time. Pantry staples vary in each household, depending on personal preference and cooking style.

I have my own set of pantry staples, but I also make an effort to avoid overstocking. It helps me keep an organized inventory of what I have. For basic needs, the following is a good foundation:

PANTRY

- Balsamic vinegar
- Black beans
- Chicken/vegetable broth
- Chickpeas
- Chipotles in adobo sauce
- Coconut milk
- Coconut oil
- Extra-virgin olive oil
- Honey
- Marinara sauce
- Onions
- Peanut butter
- Sweet potatoes

Top Five Pantry Staples

QUINOA. Quinoa is a gluten-free supergrain that I cook with all the time. In any of my recipes you can swap out the rice for quinoa. This will increase the amount of fiber and protein in the dish.

OLIVE OIL. This is easily one of the handiest items you can have in your pantry. From sautéing chicken to cooking vegetables to making salad dressings, I use it in almost every recipe.

BABY SPINACH. I love baby spinach because it's so versatile. It can easily be thrown into pasta or smoothies, or be used for salads.

BLACK BEANS. Black beans are an excellent vegetarian source of protein. I always have a couple of cans on hand to put into my salads, soups, or chili.

FROZEN MEAT. If I have to buy meat in a package, as opposed to at the meat counter, I will place the unused portion in a plastic bag and freeze it for another time. This reduces waste and gives me options when planning for future meals. I also try to have some ground beef, chicken breasts, and some sort of seafood in the freezer at all times.

DRIED GOODS

- All-purpose flour
- Bread crumbs
- Dried fruits
- Nuts
- Old-fashioned oats
- Quinoa
- Red lentils
- White rice
- White whole-wheat flour
- Whole-grain pasta

FREEZER

- Baguette
- Chocolate chips
- Frozen fruit
- Ground beef
- Mixed vegetables (peas, carrots, corn, and green beans)
- Raw chicken breasts
- Raw salmon
- Raw shrimp
- Stir-fry vegetables (onions and peppers)

REFRIGERATOR

- Almond milk
- Baby spinach
- Butter
- Dijon mustard
- Eggs
- Mayonnaise
- Plain whole-milk Greek yogurt
- Shredded cheese
- Soy sauce

COOKING EQUIPMENT

There are an endless number of kitchen gadgets a home cook can have. The truth is, many of them are unnecessary. Some items, such as a strawberry huller or a hard-boiled egg slicer, do provide convenience, but they usually just take up cabinet space. I often forget to use them when the time comes anyway! The majority of the recipes in this cookbook can be made with just a few of the cooking tools that I list here.

These aren't the only items you may need, but they're the ones you really can't live without.

Cast-iron skillet. Cast-iron skillets are the industrious powerhouse of any kitchen. The heavy-duty pan can go straight from the stove top to the oven. Their usefulness comes in handy for a multitude of recipes, such as Skillet Lasagna (page 118) and Mexican Vegetable Quinoa Skillet (page 55).

Nonstick skillet. This type of pan makes cleaning up a breeze. I prefer a nonstick skillet for making eggs because I know cleanup will be easy.

Wooden spatula. I have my fair share of rubber spatulas, but wooden spatulas hold a special place in my heart because of their versatility. They can be used for scrambling eggs, stirring soups, tossing a salad, and even making cookie dough. Don't underestimate the power of a wooden spatula.

Measuring cups. When recipes are scaled back, you often need to measure out portions of ingredients, as opposed to using an entire bag or box of ingredients. Measuring cups come in handy for every recipe in this book.

Muffin pan. Muffin pans are great for a multitude of dessert recipes, such as Raspberry Oat Cups (page 137), French Toast Muffins (page 17), and Caramel-Stuffed Brownie Bites (page 136).

STORING LEFTOVERS

This cookbook is geared toward cooking for two people, so the majority of recipes won't leave you with many—or any—leftovers. However, since portions will naturally vary from person to person, here are a few tips on storing any leftovers you may have.

Use glass containers. It sounds obvious, but glass containers make it easy to identify what kind of leftovers you have so you don't forget about them. Plus, glass makes it easy to go straight from the freezer to the microwave, as microwaving plastic should be avoided.

Use airtight containers. Store leftover desserts, such as brownies and cookies, in airtight containers so they don't get stale. (Or, if you don't anticipate eating them soon, freeze them in plastic zip-top bags for future sweet treats.) Airtight containers are also great because they allow you to avoid freezer burn. That said, freezer burn doesn't mean the food is unsafe to eat. It will simply not taste as good.

Freeze any unused raw meat. You may think that raw meat needs to be cooked right away, but that's not the case. If you find yourself with extra raw meat of any kind, immediately place it in a resealable freezer bag and freeze until you're ready to use it for another recipe.

Freeze food within two hours. Leftovers typically need to be stored in the refrigerator or freezer within two hours of being cooked before bacteria begins to grow. (As mentioned previously, the exception is raw meat, which should be frozen immediately.)

Label your leftovers. This is another one that sounds obvious, but it's so easy to forget. Place a piece of tape on your container and label it

with the contents and date so you don't have to play a guessing game in the future.

Use wide-mouth mason jars (or canning jars) to store leftover soups. Reheating soup becomes simple when you use wide-mouth mason jars. The straight sides of the jars mean that the glass will remain strong despite temperature changes, so you don't have to worry about your container cracking, melting, or worse.

Keep dressing on the side. When storing leftover salad, keep the dressing off the greens until you are ready to eat it; otherwise the salad will get soggy.

MINIMIZING WASTE

1. Plan your meals prior to grocery shopping to avoid impulse buys and overbuying.

2. Store your herbs wrapped in paper towels to keep them dry and fresh for longer.

3. Plan to bring leftovers for lunch so you actually eat them.

4. Make smart swaps in recipes by using what you already have in your pantry and refrigerator.

5. Take inventory of your pantry, refrigerator, and freezer before you go grocery shopping.

6. If you have a deep freezer or a large pantry, keep a running list of the things you store in them, so you can be sure to use them and not overbuy.

7. Store pantry goods in airtight containers to keep them fresh for as long as possible.

8. Compost any scraps when you cook.

9. Avoid clutter in your pantry, refrigerator, and freezer so you can see—and use—what you have.

10. Freeze any fruits or vegetables that seem on the verge of spoiling to preserve them. You can use these items for smoothies or soups later.

HOW TO USE THIS BOOK

In this cookbook you will find recipes that take 30 minutes or less to make, and most require eight ingredients or less. Instead of using packaged ingredients for shortcuts, I have strived to create recipes that use fresh ingredients as much as possible to create quick, delicious, and relatively healthy meals. (Exceptions include things like rice and pasta!)

My goal is that the realistic portion sizes and scaled-back recipes will be a relief for those frustrated with an abundance of leftovers, and with cookbooks where every recipe makes enough for six to eight people. You won't find any recipes that make more than three servings here.

To make cooking even easier, I've added labels to recipes with special features. Most of the recipes fall into at least one of these categories:

5-Ingredient—This means there are five or fewer ingredients in the recipe, other than salt, pepper, or olive oil.

One Pot—This label means that the recipe requires only one pot or pan for cooking. Note that this does not include the use of mixing bowls or other equipment, which are sometimes necessary additions.

Super Quick—This label means the recipe takes 20 minutes or less in total to finish.

Vegetarian—This label means the recipe does not contain meat or fish.

Vegan—This label means the recipe contains no meat, fish, dairy, or animal products.

Mango Berry Smoothies, *page 11*

CHAPTER TWO

BREAKFAST

The cliché is true: Breakfast is the most important meal of the day. The food you eat first thing in the morning sets the tone for your entire day. However, cooking for breakfast is often the most challenging because who wants to wake up earlier than necessary just to cook? These recipes range in cooking time from 5 to 30 minutes. Here you'll find everything from breakfast sandwiches and hash to cinnamon rolls and French toast.

Mango Berry Smoothies

We make smoothies almost every morning. They're so easy to make and provide an excellent means to get some fruit and veggies into your diet. This Mango Berry Smoothie is a favorite of ours.

SUPER QUICK
VEGETARIAN

PREP TIME: 5 minutes
SERVES: 2

2 cups unsweetened vanilla almond milk

1 cup frozen mixed berries

1 cup frozen mango

1 frozen banana

½ cup vanilla Greek yogurt

1 tablespoon honey, optional

1. **Combine the ingredients.** Put the almond milk, mixed berries, mango, banana, Greek yogurt, and honey (if using) in the blender.

2. **Blend.** Blend on high to purée. Pour into two glasses, serve, and enjoy.

TIP: Throw a handful of fresh spinach or kale into this smoothie for added nutrients—you won't taste it at all. You can also use fresh berries instead of frozen; just be sure to throw in a few ice cubes.

SWAP: If you don't have frozen mango, try frozen pineapple. The sweet fruit adds a clean, crisp flavor to the smoothie.

Per serving: Calories: 225; Total fat: 5g; Total carbs: 42g; Sugar: 29g; Protein: 6g; Fiber: 6g; Sodium: 194mg

Peanut Butter Banana Smoothie Bowls

On mornings when I want something more substantial than a smoothie, a smoothie bowl comes to the rescue. These bowls have a thicker consistency than smoothies, so they can be eaten with a spoon and topped with fresh fruit and granola. The combination of peanut butter and banana is a favorite of mine.

SUPER QUICK
VEGETARIAN

PREP TIME: 10 minutes
SERVES: 2

3 frozen bananas

1 cup unsweetened vanilla almond milk

4 tablespoons peanut butter, divided

2 tablespoons honey, divided

1 fresh banana, sliced

½ cup granola

2 tablespoons chia seeds, optional

1. **Combine the ingredients.** In a blender, combine the bananas, almond milk, 2 tablespoons of peanut butter, and 1 tablespoon of honey. Blend until smooth. Since this is thicker than a smoothie, you may need to stir it up a couple of times to get it well blended. Divide between two small bowls.

2. **Prepare the peanut butter topping.** In a very small microwave-safe bowl, pour the remaining 2 tablespoons of peanut butter and 1 tablespoon of honey. Stir to combine and microwave for 10 seconds.

3. **Assemble.** Top with the sliced banana, granola, and chia seeds (if using). Drizzle with the warm peanut butter and honey. Serve and enjoy.

TIP: If you want to drink this smoothie bowl instead of eat it with a spoon, add ½ cup more almond milk for a thinner consistency.

SWAP: This is the perfect recipe to experiment with other nut butters, including cashew or almond butter. Each will bring its own distinct, nutty flavor to the smoothie bowls, and you may find out you like one more than the other. Other topping ideas include berries, chocolate chips, chopped peanuts, ground flaxseed, and shredded coconut.

Per serving: Calories: 552; Total fat: 33g; Total carbs: 111g; Sugar: 62g; Protein: 20g; Fiber: 14g; Sodium: 255mg

Cinnamon-Apple Yogurt Parfaits

Yogurt is a no-brainer when it comes to quick and easy breakfasts, but this recipe takes things up a notch. A quick sauté of the cinnamon apples and some granola are all it takes to turn your plain bowl of yogurt into a parfait.

SUPER QUICK
VEGETARIAN

PREP TIME: 10 minutes
COOK TIME: 10 minutes
SERVES: 2

1 tablespoon butter

1 large apple, peeled, cored, and diced

1 teaspoon ground cinnamon, divided

1 teaspoon vanilla extract

1½ cups plain Greek yogurt

2 tablespoons honey

½ cup vanilla granola

1. **Cook the apple.** In a medium skillet over medium heat, melt the butter. Add the apple and ½ teaspoon of cinnamon. Cook until the apple is softened, about 10 minutes.

2. **Prepare the yogurt.** Meanwhile, combine the Greek yogurt, vanilla extract, the remaining ½ teaspoon of cinnamon, and honey in a bowl, and stir to combine.

3. **Assemble the parfaits.** Divide the yogurt between two bowls and top with the apple. Top with the granola. Serve and enjoy.

SWAP: Use maple syrup or agave instead of honey. Regular plain yogurt will also work well in this recipe.

Per serving: Calories: 354; Total fat: 10g; Total carbs: 49g; Sugar: 37g; Protein: 19g; Fiber: 4g; Sodium: 127mg

3-Minute Microwave Vanilla Almond Granola

Granola cooked in 3 minutes might seem too good to be true, but it really does work. Use this recipe as a starting point, and customize with your favorite add-ins. Serve with milk, on top of yogurt, or on top of smoothies.

SUPER QUICK
VEGETARIAN

PREP TIME: 10 minutes
COOK TIME: 3 minutes
SERVES: 2

3 teaspoons coconut oil

2 teaspoons water

¼ teaspoon vanilla extract

2 teaspoons maple syrup

⅓ cup old-fashioned oats

2 tablespoons sliced almonds

1 tablespoon dried cranberries

1. **Combine the wet ingredients.** In a microwave-safe bowl or mason jar, mix the coconut oil, water, vanilla, and maple syrup. Microwave on high for 20 seconds, or until the coconut oil is melted.

2. **Add the dry ingredients.** In the same bowl or jar, add the oats and almonds, and stir to combine. Microwave on high for 1 to 2 minutes, stirring every 30 seconds, until the oats begin to brown.

3. **Cool the granola.** Spread the granola out onto a plate to cool off. Add the dried cranberries once it's cool. Serve and enjoy.

TIP: Be sure to add the dried cranberries after the microwaving process; otherwise they'll burn.

SWAP: You can customize this granola to your liking by choosing different dried fruits and nuts. Dried apricots, raisins, dried bananas, peanuts, pistachios, and cashews are all good choices.

Per serving: Calories: 182; Total fat: 11g; Total carbs: 22g; Sugar: 13g; Protein: 2g; Fiber: 2g; Sodium: 3mg

Crescent Roll Cinnamon Rolls

Is there anything more comforting on a weekend morning than a pan of cinnamon rolls? Making them from scratch can be a time-consuming and laborious process. On some mornings I don't mind taking the time, but on other mornings I don't want to wait. I often allow myself the cheat of using a can of crescent rolls to speed up the process, so I can still delight in the soft, flaky dough.

VEGETARIAN

PREP TIME: 10 minutes
COOK TIME: 15 minutes
SERVES: 2

Nonstick cooking spray

1 (4-ounce) can crescent rolls

1 tablespoon butter, melted

1 teaspoon cinnamon

2 tablespoons brown sugar

1 teaspoon maple syrup

½ tablespoon milk

⅓ cup powdered sugar

1. **Prepare.** Preheat the oven to 350°F. Lightly coat four cavities of a muffin pan with nonstick cooking spray.

2. **Prep the crescent rolls.** Take the crescent roll dough out of the tube and lay it flat on a work surface. Pinch the seams together. Flip the dough over and pinch the seams together on the other side, as well. Brush the resulting rectangle with the melted butter, then sprinkle with the cinnamon and brown sugar. Roll the dough into a log.

3. **Cut.** Cut the log into 4 cinnamon rolls.

4. **Assemble.** Place each cinnamon roll into the prepared muffin pan.

5. **Bake.** Bake for 10 to 12 minutes, until golden.

6. **Prepare the glaze.** While the rolls are baking, mix the maple syrup, milk, and powdered sugar in a small bowl.

7. **Glaze the rolls.** Drizzle the glaze over the warm cinnamon rolls and serve immediately.

SWAP: For a lemon roll, use the zest from half a lemon or instead of the cinnamon.

Per serving: Calories: 396; Total fat: 18g; Total carbs: 54g; Sugar: 34g; Protein: 4g; Fiber: 1g; Sodium: 486mg

Blender Peanut Butter–Banana–Chocolate Chip Muffins

Every time I make these muffins, I can't believe how easy they are to prepare. You simply put everything but the chocolate chips in the blender, and mix it all up. They're so tasty that you'd never guess they're flourless.

VEGETARIAN

PREP TIME: 10 minutes
COOK TIME: 20 minutes
SERVES: 2 or 3

Nonstick cooking spray

1 ripe banana

1¼ cups
old-fashioned oats

1 large egg

¼ cup maple syrup

¼ cup creamy
peanut butter

¼ cup unsweetened
vanilla almond milk

1 teaspoon
baking powder

¼ teaspoon salt

¼ cup dark
chocolate chips

1. **Prepare.** Preheat the oven to 375°F. Lightly coat a muffin pan with nonstick cooking spray.

2. **Combine the ingredients.** In a blender, combine the banana, oats, egg, maple syrup, peanut butter, almond milk, baking powder, and salt. Blend on high for 30 seconds, until well combined.

3. **Assemble the muffins.** Fill six of the muffin cups three fourths of the way full with batter. Sprinkle the chocolate chips on top.

4. **Bake.** Bake them in the preheated oven for 18 to 20 minutes, until the muffins have a dome top and are cooked through.

5. **Cool.** Cool the muffins for at least 10 minutes. Serve and enjoy.

SWAP: For a change in flavor, use almond butter instead of peanut butter. Almonds have a more delicate, nutty flavor than peanuts, which will allow the chocolate to stand out.

Per serving: Calories: 552; Total fat: 25g; Total carbs: 75g; Sugar: 42g; Protein: 16g; Fiber: 6g; Sodium: 504mg

French Toast Muffins

These French toast muffins are perfect for when you're craving French toast but don't want to stand over the stove for too long. With this recipe, you simply mix it all up, fill your muffin pan, and let the oven do the work. Drizzle your muffins with real maple syrup for the full French toast experience.

VEGETARIAN

PREP TIME: 10 minutes
COOK TIME: 20 minutes
SERVES: 2

Nonstick cooking spray

4 thick slices bread

2 large eggs

¾ cup milk

1 teaspoon pure vanilla extract

2 tablespoons sugar, divided

¼ teaspoon cinnamon

Maple syrup, optional

1. **Prepare.** Preheat the oven to 375°F and lightly coat six cavities of a muffin pan with nonstick cooking spray.

2. **Prepare the bread.** Slice the bread into 1-inch chunks and put them into a medium bowl.

3. **Combine the wet ingredients.** In a small bowl, whisk together the eggs, milk, vanilla, 1 tablespoon of sugar, and the cinnamon. Pour over the bread and stir well to combine.

4. **Assemble the muffins.** Spoon the bread mixture into the muffin cups, packing gently to fill each cavity, and sprinkle the remaining 1 tablespoon of sugar over the muffins.

5. **Bake.** Bake in the preheated oven for 15 to 18 minutes.

6. **Drizzle.** Drizzle with maple syrup, if desired, and serve.

TIP: These muffins are a great way to use day-old dry bread.

SWAP: For more decadent muffins, use brioche bread and heavy cream instead of regular bread and milk.

Per serving: Calories: 364; Total fat: 7g; Total carbs: 57g; Sugar: 17g; Protein: 16g; Fiber: 1g; Sodium: 113mg

Orange-Almond French Toast

French toast is a great dish for small-batch cooking, since you can easily control how many slices you make. Anyone can make regular old French toast, but the addition of almond extract and orange zest makes this version extra special.

VEGETARIAN

PREP TIME: 15 minutes
COOK TIME: 10 minutes
SERVES: 2

2 large eggs

⅓ cup milk

½ teaspoon almond extract

1 teaspoon grated orange zest

Pinch salt

2 tablespoons unsalted butter

4 thick slices day-old baguette

Maple syrup or powdered sugar, for serving

1. **Prepare the egg mixture.** In a shallow bowl, whisk together the eggs, milk, almond extract, orange zest, and salt.

2. **Melt the butter.** In a large skillet over medium-low heat, melt the butter.

3. **Prepare the French toast.** Dip each slice of bread into the egg mixture, coating each side.

4. **Cook the French toast.** Immediately place the soaked bread into the preheated skillet and cook for 4 to 5 minutes on each side, until golden brown.

5. **Top it off.** Top with the maple syrup or powdered sugar. Serve and enjoy.

TIP: A nonstick pan will work best for this recipe. When making the French toast, you want to cook it low and slow so each slice is cooked through and browns evenly.

SWAP: If you don't have a baguette, you can use brioche, challah, or sourdough bread. You can also use unsweetened almond milk or coconut milk instead of cow's milk.

Per serving: Calories: 442; Tot al fat: 21g; Total carbs: 60g; Sugar: 30g; Protein: 10g; Fiber: 4g; Sodium: 552mg

Caramelized Banana Pancakes

Whenever I make these, I think of the song "Banana Pancakes" by Jack Johnson, and I can't help but hum it while I cook. When I cook these pancakes, I sauté slices of banana in butter and brown sugar, which transforms them into something sweet and decadent.

VEGETARIAN

PREP TIME: 20 minutes
COOK TIME: 10 minutes
SERVES: 2

3 tablespoons
butter, divided

1 tablespoon
brown sugar

1 banana, sliced

1 cup all-purpose flour

2 tablespoons
granulated sugar

1 teaspoon
baking powder

½ teaspoon salt

1 cup buttermilk

1 large egg

1 teaspoon pure
vanilla extract

Maple syrup, for serving

1. **Caramelize the bananas.** In a small skillet over medium-high heat, melt 1 tablespoon of butter. Add the brown sugar, whisking until the sugar and butter have combined. Add the banana slices to the skillet and cook until they are caramelized on one side, about 2 minutes. Flip and cook on other side, another 2 minutes.

2. **Preheat the griddle or skillet.** Preheat an electric griddle to 350°F or place a medium skillet over medium heat.

3. **Prepare the pancakes.** In a medium bowl, whisk together the flour, granulated sugar, baking powder, and salt. In a small microwave-safe bowl, microwave the remaining 2 tablespoons of butter on high for 20 seconds or until melted. Add the buttermilk, egg, and vanilla to the melted butter and whisk together. Add the wet ingredients to the dry ingredients and stir with a spatula until combined.

4. **Cook the pancakes.** Lightly grease the preheated griddle or skillet, and drop about ⅓ cup of the batter in. Cook until bubbles begin to form and the edges begin to set. Flip and cook for another 1 to 2 minutes.

5. **Top it off.** Top the pancakes with caramelized bananas and maple syrup, and serve immediately.

SWAP: If you want to add more whole grains to your diet, try this recipe with whole-wheat flour. You can also try this recipe with other fruit, such as apples or peaches.

Per serving: Calories: 588; Total fat: 22g; Total carbs: 85g; Sugar: 30g; Protein: 15g; Fiber: 3g; Sodium: 873mg

Sweet Potato and Bacon Hash

This is my go-to weekend breakfast. We love bacon in our household, so we always have that on hand. Many times I will use whatever vegetables I have left over from the week in our refrigerator, but the sweet potato and kale in this version is my favorite combination.

PREP TIME: 10 minutes
COOK TIME: 20 minutes
SERVES: 2

3 slices bacon, cut into small pieces

1 shallot, diced

1 medium sweet potato, peeled and cut into ½-inch dice

2 garlic cloves, minced

3 large Tuscan kale leaves, stemmed and chopped

½ teaspoon salt

¼ teaspoon freshly ground black pepper

2 eggs

1. **Cook the bacon.** In an 8- or 9-inch cast-iron skillet over medium-high heat, cook the bacon until crispy, about 5 minutes. Remove from the skillet, leaving about 2 tablespoons of bacon grease in the skillet.

2. **Cook the vegetables.** Add the shallot, sweet potato, and garlic. Cook until the sweet potato is softened, about 10 minutes.

3. **Cook the kale.** Add the kale to the skillet and stir to combine with the other ingredients. Add the salt and pepper.

4. **Cook the eggs.** Crack the eggs into a small nonstick skillet over medium-high heat. Cook the eggs for 1 to 2 minutes on each side, until they reach the desired consistency.

5. **Serve.** Divide the hash between two plates and top with the eggs. Serve immediately.

TIP: I love using fresh garlic, but always keep a jar of minced garlic in my refrigerator for when I am short on time.

SWAP: Use spinach instead of kale if that's what you have on hand. It won't require quite as long a cooking time, as spinach is much more delicate than kale. Nutritionally, kale has more calcium than spinach, and spinach has more iron than kale. It's fair to say they're both nutritional powerhouses.

Per serving: Calories: 327; Total fat: 16g; Total carbs: 25g; Sugar: 4g; Protein: 21g; Fiber: 4g; Sodium: 1367mg

Southwestern Chorizo and Hash Browns

Chorizo is my favorite breakfast meat. It adds a bit of Mexican flavor and spice to any dish. These hash browns are one of my husband's favorites—he likes them extra crispy!

ONE POT

PREP TIME: 10 minutes
COOK TIME: 20 minutes
SERVES: 2

1 avocado, halved

2 tablespoons canola oil

2 cups shredded hash browns (fresh or frozen)

½ teaspoon chili powder

8 ounces chorizo sausage

1 red bell pepper, stemmed, seeded, and diced

1 small white onion, diced

2 large eggs

2 tablespoons chopped fresh cilantro

1. **Prepare the avocado.** With a sharp knife, halve the avocado lengthwise. Using a spoon, remove the pit, then remove the flesh from the peel. Cut into bite-size slices.

2. **Heat the oil.** In a large skillet over medium-high heat, heat the canola oil.

3. **Cook the hash browns.** Add the hash browns to the skillet. Cook until crispy, flipping occasionally, about 10 minutes total. Remove from the skillet.

4. **Cook the chorizo.** Add the chorizo, bell pepper, and onion to the skillet. Break the chorizo into small chunks, and cook until the meat is browned and the vegetables are softened, 7 to 8 minutes. Transfer to a plate.

5. **Cook the eggs.** Add the eggs to the skillet and cook for 1 to 2 minutes on each side, or until they reach the desired consistency.

6. **Serve.** Divide the hash browns between two plates and top each plate with half of the chorizo-vegetable mixture and 1 egg. Top with the sliced avocado and chopped cilantro, and serve.

TIP: You could also try scrambled or poached eggs instead.

SWAP: Not everyone loves spicy food, so you can use breakfast sausage in place of chorizo if you want to tone down the peppery heat.

Per serving: Calories: 869; Total fat: 67g; Total carbs: 41g; Sugar: 8g; Protein: 30g; Fiber: 9g; Sodium: 829mg

Egg Pesto Mozzarella Sandwich

Who says pesto is only for pasta? These breakfast sandwiches are lightened up, meatless, and still full of flavor! I like my egg yolks runny, but if you prefer them cooked through, just cook the eggs a minute longer on each side or scramble them.

5-INGREDIENT
SUPER QUICK
VEGETARIAN

PREP TIME: 10 minutes
COOK TIME: 10 minutes
SERVES: 2

Nonstick cooking spray

2 large eggs

4 ounces fresh mozzarella cheese, sliced and divided

¼ cup pesto

1 small tomato, sliced

2 ciabatta buns

1. **Preheat the broiler.**

2. **Cook the eggs.** Lightly coat a nonstick skillet over medium-high heat with nonstick cooking spray. Add the eggs and cook for 1 to 2 minutes on each side, until the egg whites are cooked but the yolk is still runny.

3. **Prep the sandwiches.** Cut the ciabatta buns in half and place the bottom portions on a baking sheet. Place half of the mozzarella cheese on the bottom slices. Spread the pesto on the top halves and place them cut-side up on the baking sheet.

4. **Broil the cheese.** Broil the buns for 1 to 2 minutes, until the cheese is melted and the pesto is warm.

5. **Assemble.** Place 1 egg on each bottom bun. Top with another slice of mozzarella cheese and some tomato slices. Place the other side of each bun on top and serve immediately.

TIP: You can turn this dish into a panini-style sandwich by using whole-grain or sourdough bread. Just spread a little butter on each side, then place on a skillet over medium-high heat for 3 to 4 minutes on each side before assembling.

SWAP: Instead of tomato and pesto, try fresh basil leaves and roasted red bell pepper. The sweet basil and smoky pepper combine beautifully in this sandwich.

Per serving: Calories: 544; Total fat: 33g; Total carbs: 35g; Sugar: 6g; Protein: 27g; Fiber: 3g; Sodium: 827mg

BLT Avocado Toast

At the risk of sounding like a cliché millennial, I'm going to admit that I am obsessed with avocado toast. Some mornings I just sprinkle sea salt and lemon juice on my mashed avocado, but when I'm feeling like something more substantial, this BLT Avocado Toast is a great option.

SUPER QUICK

PREP TIME: 10 minutes
COOK TIME: 10 minutes
SERVES: 2

4 slices bacon

1 avocado

Juice of ½ lemon

Pinch sea salt

Pinch freshly ground black pepper

1 tomato, sliced

¼ cup arugula

4 slices whole-grain toast

1. **Cook the bacon.** In a medium skillet over medium-high heat, cook the bacon for 5 to 7 minutes or until it reaches your preferred texture.

2. **Prepare the avocado.** While the bacon is cooking, peel and pit the avocado. In a small bowl, mash the avocado, add the lemon juice, and season with salt and pepper.

3. **Assemble.** Spread each piece of toast with mashed avocado. Top with the bacon, tomato, and arugula. Serve and enjoy.

TIP: For an extra protein boost, top the avocado toast with a fried egg.

SWAP: Arugula has a bit of bite to it. If you're not a fan, use baby spinach in its place.

Per serving: Calories: 500; Total fat: 32g; Total carbs: 32g; Sugar: 5g; Protein: 23g; Fiber: 10g; Sodium: 1228mg

Denver Omelet Scramble

I'm not super comfortable making omelets—the flipping part makes me nervous. Still, I love a good Denver omelet, so I turned it into a hash instead. This hash has all of the flavors without the stress-inducing flip!

ONE POT

PREP TIME: 10 minutes
COOK TIME: 15 minutes
SERVES: 2

2 tablespoons butter

1 small russet potato, diced

½ green bell pepper, seeded and diced

½ red bell pepper, seeded and diced

½ small white onion, diced

4 large eggs

¼ cup milk

Salt

Freshly ground black pepper

½ cup diced ham

½ cup cheddar cheese

1. **Cook the vegetables.** In a medium skillet over medium-high heat, melt the butter. Add the potato, bell peppers, and onion. Cook until the potato is softened, about 10 minutes.

2. **Prepare the eggs.** While the vegetables are cooking, in a small bowl, whisk together the eggs and milk, and season with salt and pepper.

3. **Cook the ham.** Add the ham to the vegetables and cook for another 2 minutes.

4. **Cook the eggs.** Reduce the heat to low and add the egg mixture, stirring to combine with the vegetables and ham. Cook until the eggs are scrambled and no longer wet, stirring often, about 5 minutes. Stir in the cheese. Then serve and enjoy.

TIP: Use your leftover bell peppers to make Hawaiian Steak Kabobs (page 110)!

SWAP: Use a sweet potato instead of a russet potato for a healthy dose of beta-carotene.

Per serving: Calories: 522; Total fat: 35g; Total carbs: 25g; Sugar: 4g; Protein: 29g; Fiber: 3g; Sodium: 858mg

Mexican Breakfast Bowls

It's no secret that I love Mexican food; I'm always looking for ways to bring Mexican flavors into my breakfast. This recipe also reveals my secret to the fluffiest scrambled eggs: whole-milk Greek yogurt. It's a trick that I learned from my dad, and I've never made scrambled eggs without it since. These breakfast bowls are incredibly hearty, healthy, and a great way to power up for the day.

SUPER QUICK

PREP TIME: 10 minutes
COOK TIME: 10 minutes
SERVES: 2

4 large eggs

2 tablespoons plain whole-milk Greek yogurt

¼ teaspoon salt

Pinch freshly ground black pepper

1 cup canned black beans, drained and rinsed

½ teaspoon cumin

1 cup pico de gallo

½ avocado, peeled, pitted, and sliced

2 tablespoons chopped fresh cilantro

½ cup shredded cheddar cheese

1. **Prepare the eggs.** In a medium bowl, whisk together the eggs and yogurt, and season with the salt and pepper.

2. **Cook the eggs.** In a medium skillet over medium-low heat, melt the butter and add the eggs. Cook slowly, stirring with a rubber spatula frequently, until the eggs are scrambled and no longer wet.

3. **Warm the black beans.** Add the black beans and cumin to a microwave-safe bowl and microwave for 1 minute, until warm.

4. **Assemble.** Assemble the breakfast bowls by dividing the eggs and black beans between two bowls. Top with the pico de gallo, avocado, cilantro, and cheese. Serve and enjoy.

TIP: The key to creating these fluffy eggs is the cooking temperature. A burner on medium-low heat will result in a soft and fluffy scrambled egg every time.

SWAP: If you find Greek yogurt to be too tangy, try sour cream instead. The consistency and fat content are about the same, but sour cream offers a subtler flavor.

Per serving: Calories: 551; Total fat: 29g; Total carbs: 43g; Sugar: 2g; Protein: 29g; Fiber: 11g; Sodium: 1162mg

Bacon, Brie, and Raspberry Jam Grilled Cheese Sandwiches, *page 39*

CHAPTER THREE

SOUPS, SALADS, AND SANDWICHES

Not every meal has to be fancy. Sometimes a simple soup, salad, or sandwich does the trick. However, that doesn't mean your meals have to be boring, either. Each of the dishes in this chapter is full of flavor. I've created recipes here for every season, from a Summer Vegetable Salad (page 32) to a cozy winter Sausage and Tortellini Soup (page 44).

Melon and Cucumber Salad

This summery salad is light, crisp, and refreshing. The cucumber brings a bit of savory flavor to the dish, and the lime and mint brighten it up even more. On a hot summer night, all you need is this salad and a spot on your patio.

SUPER QUICK
VEGETARIAN

PREP TIME: 15 minutes
SERVES: 2 or 3

1 cup cubed cantaloupe

1 cup cubed watermelon

1 small cucumber, peeled and diced

Zest and juice of ½ lime

2 tablespoons chopped fresh mint

1 teaspoon extra-virgin olive oil

¼ cup feta cheese

1. **Combine the ingredients.** In a medium bowl, combine the cantaloupe, watermelon, cucumber, lime zest, lime juice, mint, and olive oil, and mix.

2. **Garnish.** Top with the feta cheese. Serve and enjoy.

TIP: While a melon baller will create perfect bite-size pieces, it's a tool that is not necessary. Cutting the melon into bite-size cubes will work just as well.

SWAP: Honeydew or any other type of melon that you like will make an excellent substitution in place of the cantaloupe and watermelon.

Per serving: Calories: 154; Total fat: 7g; Total carbs: 22g; Sugar: 15g; Protein: 5g; Fiber: 3g; Sodium: 223mg

Grapefruit-Avocado Salad

This salad is the perfect example of how the simplest ingredients can combine to make the most delicious dish. Prepare this salad when grapefruits are in season for the most flavorful results.

5-INGREDIENT
SUPER QUICK

PREP TIME: 20 minutes
SERVES: 2

1 ruby grapefruit

1 ripe avocado

1 tablespoon extra-virgin olive oil

½ tablespoon white wine vinegar

1 teaspoon honey

1 small shallot, diced

Pinch salt

Pinch freshly ground black pepper

1. **Prepare the grapefruit and avocado.** Using your fingers, peel the grapefruit. With a sharp knife, carefully cut between the membranes to remove the grapefruit sections. Cut the avocado in half. Remove the pit. Remove the flesh from the skin using a spoon and cut into slices. Arrange the avocado and grapefruit on a plate or in a bowl in alternating slices.

2. **Make the vinaigrette.** In a small mason jar, combine the olive oil, white wine vinegar, honey, shallot, salt, and pepper. Stir with a whisk or cover with a lid and shake to combine.

3. **Assemble the salad.** Pour the vinaigrette over the avocado and grapefruit, and toss to combine. Serve and enjoy.

TIP: Figuring out which avocado is ripe can be challenging. I like to give it a little squeeze—it should have some give, but not too much. Another indicator is the stem. If an avocado isn't too ripe you should be able to peel off the stem, and underneath you should see green, not brown.

SWAP: No grapefruit around? You can use an orange instead. An orange will bring a little more sweetness to the dish, but the citrus will still pair nicely with the avocado.

Per serving: Calories: 240; Total fat: 20g; Total carbs: 16g; Sugar: 8g; Protein: 2g; Fiber: 7g; Sodium: 85mg

Beet and Goat Cheese Arugula Salad

This salad is for all the beet lovers out there. It combines the earthy flavor of beets with peppery arugula and tangy goat cheese, and the end result is delicious.

VEGETARIAN

PREP TIME: 5 minutes
COOK TIME: 25 minutes
SERVES: 2

3 medium beets

1 tablespoon extra-virgin olive oil, plus ¼ cup

Salt

Freshly ground black pepper

2 tablespoons balsamic vinegar

1 shallot, finely diced

1 tablespoon honey

3 ounces fresh arugula

¼ cup slivered almonds

2 to 3 ounces fresh soft goat cheese, crumbled

1. **Prepare.** Preheat the oven to 450°F.

2. **Prepare the beets.** Using a knife, cut the skin off the beets, then cut off each end. Cut each beet into quarters and then cut the quarters into ½-inch-thick pieces. Place the beets on a baking sheet. Drizzle with 1 tablespoon of olive oil, and season with salt and pepper.

3. **Roast the beets.** Roast for 20 to 25 minutes, until tender.

4. **Prepare the dressing.** While the beets are roasting, whisk together the balsamic vinegar, shallot, honey, and remaining ¼ cup of extra-virgin olive oil in a small bowl.

5. **Assemble the salads.** Divide the arugula between two plates and top with the beets, almonds, and goat cheese.

6. **Dress the salad.** Drizzle the dressing over the salads and toss. Serve and enjoy.

TIP: Cutting your beets into bite-size pieces before roasting will keep the cook time to a minimum.

SWAP: If goat cheese isn't one of your favorites, try feta cheese or Parmesan cheese instead. These types of salty cheeses contrast nicely with sweetness of the beets.

Per serving: Calories: 476; Total fat: 38g; Total carbs: 29g; Sugar: 22g; Protein: 12g; Fiber: 5g; Sodium: 233mg

Summer Vegetable Salad

I love to make this salad in the summertime, especially when the tomatoes I've planted are ripe and the basil in my garden is overflowing. This salad is fresh, fast, delicious, and a great addition to an outdoor barbecue or picnic.

SUPER QUICK
VEGETARIAN

PREP TIME: 15 minutes
COOK TIME: 3 minutes
SERVES: 2 or 3

2 ears sweet corn

1 Roma tomato, diced

1 small cucumber, diced

½ small red onion, thinly sliced

2 tablespoons chopped fresh basil

¼ cup feta cheese

1 tablespoon extra-virgin olive oil

¼ teaspoon salt

¼ teaspoon freshly ground black pepper

1. **Cook the corn.** Place the unshucked corn in the microwave, and cook for 3 minutes. Let it cool slightly. Shuck the husks off the cobs and cut the corn kernels off into a medium bowl.

2. **Assemble the salad.** In the same bowl, add the tomato, cucumber, onion, basil, feta cheese, and olive oil, and toss to combine. Season with the salt and pepper. Serve and enjoy.

TIP: Microwaving your sweet corn is the fastest and easiest way to cook it. If you have a little extra time, brush it with olive oil and cook it on a grill pan for about 5 minutes, turning every minute or so.

SWAP: You can use whatever variety of tomato is your favorite, or whatever you grow in your garden or find at the farmers' market.

Per serving: Calories: 303; Total fat: 14g; Total carbs: 44g; Sugar: 17g; Protein: 10g; Fiber: 6g; Sodium: 536mg

Kale Caesar Salad

In recent years, kale has become *the* dark green leafy vegetable. I've wholeheartedly jumped on the bandwagon and use it any chance I get. My husband is a little more reluctant to embrace kale, but he really loves this salad. The trick is to use a combination of kale and romaine lettuce. I also like to make my own croutons for this dish, using day-old bread.

PREP TIME: 15 minutes
COOK TIME: 10 minutes
SERVES: 2

1 cup cubed baguette

2 tablespoons extra-virgin olive oil, plus ¼ cup

Salt

Freshly ground black pepper

2 teaspoons Dijon mustard

2 teaspoons Worcestershire sauce

½ teaspoon hot sauce

2 teaspoons anchovy paste

1 cup grated Parmesan cheese, divided

1 bunch Tuscan kale, stemmed and finely chopped

1 head romaine lettuce, chopped

1. **Prepare and make the croutons.** Preheat the oven to 400°F. In a medium bowl, toss the bread cubes with 2 tablespoons of olive oil, and season with salt and pepper. Place them on a baking sheet and bake for 10 minutes.

2. **Make the dressing.** In a small bowl, whisk together the remaining ¼ cup of olive oil, Dijon mustard, Worcestershire sauce, hot sauce, anchovy paste, and ½ cup of the Parmesan cheese.

3. **Assemble the salad.** In a medium bowl, combine the kale and romaine. Drizzle the dressing and stir well for at least 2 minutes to incorporate the dressing into the leaves. Let sit for 5 to 10 minutes.

4. **Serve.** Top with the remaining ½ cup of Parmesan cheese and croutons. Serve and enjoy.

TIP: This makes a great vegetarian salad (if you leave out the anchovy paste), but you can also top it with grilled steak, shrimp, or chicken for a protein boost.

SWAP: Omit the anchovy paste if you can't find it or don't care for the salty, oily fish. You can also use bagged croutons if you don't want to make them.

Per serving: Calories: 619; Total fat: 48g; Total carbs: 40g; Sugar: 4g; Protein: 27g; Fiber: 4g; Sodium: 1252mg

Zucchini and Corn Panzanella Salad

I first had a panzanella salad a few years ago at an Italian restaurant, and was immediately hooked. In the winter I like to make this bread salad with roasted squash and pumpkin seeds, and in the summer I prefer to add fresh vegetables, such as this zucchini and corn version.

VEGETARIAN

PREP TIME: 10 minutes
COOK TIME: 20 minutes
SERVES: 2 or 3

1 small baguette

4 tablespoons extra-virgin olive oil, divided

Salt

Freshly ground black pepper

1 zucchini

½ cup frozen corn

½ tablespoon Dijon mustard

1 tablespoon red wine vinegar

1 tablespoon chopped fresh chives

¼ cup shredded Parmesan cheese

1. **Prepare and bake the bread cubes.** Preheat the oven to 400°F. Cut the baguette into 1-inch cubes and put into a medium bowl. Toss with 2 tablespoons of olive oil and season with salt and pepper. Spread the bread cubes on a baking sheet and bake for 10 minutes.

2. **Prepare the zucchini.** While the bread is toasting, halve the zucchini lengthwise, then cut into half rounds about ¼ inch thick.

3. **Cook the zucchini and corn.** In a medium skillet over medium-high heat, heat 1 tablespoon of olive oil. Add the zucchini and corn, and cook until the zucchini is softened and the corn is cooked through, about 10 minutes. Season with salt and pepper.

4. **Make the dressing.** While the zucchini and corn are cooking, prepare the dressing. Combine the remaining 1 tablespoon of olive oil with the Dijon mustard, vinegar, and chives in a small mason jar, and shake well to combine.

5. **Assemble the salad.** In a medium bowl, combine the toasted bread cubes, zucchini, corn, and Parmesan. Toss with the dressing, then season with salt and pepper. Serve and enjoy.

TIP: Grilling both the bread and the vegetables is worth-while. The cooking process brings a nice smoky richness to the salad. For the bread, place the cubes on a grill pan over medium-high flame and toast for 5 minutes. For the veggies, place them on that same grill and cook for 10 minutes.

SWAP: Any sturdy vegetable is a good choice for this dish. I like asparagus sometimes instead of zucchini. Red bell peppers, eggplant, or even tomatoes also work well in this salad.

Per serving: Calories: 477; Total fat: 33g; Total carbs: 39g; Sugar: 4g; Protein: 13g; Fiber: 4g; Sodium: 580mg

Grilled Romaine with Buttermilk Dressing

It might seem strange to grill romaine lettuce, but trust me on this one. Just a minute or two on the grill is all it takes, and you'll never want to eat a regular romaine salad again. This recipe is great for two people since all you need is one romaine head to split.

SUPER QUICK
VEGETARIAN

PREP TIME: 15 minutes
COOK TIME: 2 minutes
SERVES: 2

¼ cup buttermilk

¼ cup mayonnaise

1 tablespoon chopped fresh chives

1 tablespoon chopped fresh dill

1 scallion, finely chopped

1 garlic clove, minced

¼ teaspoon salt

1 head romaine lettuce

1 tablespoon extra-virgin olive oil

¼ cup shaved Parmesan cheese

1. **Prepare.** Preheat the grill to medium-high heat.

2. **Make the buttermilk dressing.** In a small bowl, combine the buttermilk, mayonnaise, chives, dill, scallion, garlic, and salt. Whisk, then set aside.

3. **Prepare the romaine.** Cut the romaine lettuce head in half lengthwise. Brush the halves with the olive oil.

4. **Grill the romaine.** Place the romaine on the preheated grill, cut-side down. Grill for 1 to 2 minutes with grill lid closed, or until the lettuce is lightly charred.

5. **Dress the salad.** Drizzle with the buttermilk dressing and sprinkle with the shaved Parmesan cheese. Serve and enjoy.

SWAP: You can make this dish vegan by omitting the cheese and making a vegan dressing. For the dressing, simply use avocado oil mayonnaise instead of regular mayonnaise, and ¼ cup unsweetened almond milk plus 1 tablespoon of lemon juice instead of buttermilk. Add the same amounts of chives, dill scallion, garlic, and salt to the dressing, and whisk.

Per serving: Calories: 256; Total fat: 20g; Total carbs: 15g; Sugar: 5g; Protein: 6g; Fiber: 1g; Sodium: 712mg

Curried Avocado Chickpea Salad

I am always on the hunt for new lunch ideas. If you find that you tend to get stuck in the typical rut of having the same salads or sandwiches for lunch for days on end, this chickpea salad is the cure!

SUPER QUICK
VEGETARIAN

PREP TIME: 15 minutes
SERVES: 2 or 3

1 (15-ounce) can chickpeas, drained and rinsed

1 ripe avocado, peeled, pitted, and diced

1 tablespoon plain Greek yogurt

2 tablespoons chopped fresh cilantro

1 scallion, chopped

1 teaspoon curry powder

½ teaspoon turmeric

¼ teaspoon salt

¼ teaspoon freshly ground black pepper

Pita bread and salad greens, optional

1. **Combine the ingredients.** In a medium bowl, combine the chickpeas, avocado, Greek yogurt, cilantro, scallion, curry powder, turmeric, salt, and pepper.

2. **Serve.** Place this mixture on top of salad greens or in pita bread, if desired, or eat it by itself. Serve and enjoy.

TIP: If you're making this into a sandwich, mash the chickpeas and avocado together so it's easier to spread and eat.

SWAP: If plain Greek yogurt doesn't appeal to your taste buds, try sour cream or mayonnaise instead.

Per serving: Calories: 438; Total fat: 16g; Total carbs: 63g; Sugar: 1g; Protein: 14g; Fiber: 17g; Sodium: 1017mg

Cherry-Pecan Chicken Salad

In high school I worked at a popular sandwich shop, and my favorite thing to order on my lunch break was the chicken salad on a croissant. I still dream of it today. This Cherry Pecan Chicken Salad is the closest I have come to replicating my favorite lunch dish. It hits the spot every time. I still love my chicken salad on a croissant, but any bread—or even a pile of greens—will do.

ONE POT
SUPER QUICK

PREP TIME: 10 minutes
COOK TIME: 10 minutes
SERVES: 2

2 boneless skinless
chicken breasts

¼ cup mayonnaise

¼ cup plain Greek yogurt
or sour cream

1 shallot, diced

1 celery stalk, diced

½ cup chopped pecans

¼ cup dried cherries

Salt

Freshly ground
black pepper

1. **Cook the chicken.** Fill a medium pot halfway with water and place over high heat. As the water heats up, cut each chicken breast into two pieces. Add the chicken to the pot and boil until cooked through, about 10 minutes. Using tongs, remove the chicken from the water and shred or chop into bite-size pieces.

2. **Assemble.** In a medium bowl, combine the chicken, mayonnaise, Greek yogurt, shallot, celery, pecans, and cherries. Season with salt and pepper. Serve and enjoy.

TIP: Use shredded rotisserie chicken to save yourself time.

SWAP: You can use dried cranberries instead of dried cherries or almonds instead of pecans.

Per serving: Calories: 379; Total fat: 24g; Total carbs: 15g; Sugar: 5g; Protein: 26g; Fiber: 2g; Sodium: 367mg

Bacon, Brie, and Raspberry Jam Grilled Cheese Sandwiches

My mom was the inspiration for these sandwiches. She told me about one dreary spring day when this sandwich was the perfect comfort food to lift her mood. I couldn't stop thinking about the combination, and as it turns out, these are over-the-top delicious!

5-INGREDIENT

PREP TIME: 10 minutes
COOK TIME: 20 minutes
SERVES: 2

4 slices bacon
4 slices sourdough bread
1 tablespoon butter
6 thick slices Brie
2 tablespoons raspberry jam

1. **Cook the bacon.** In a medium skillet over medium-high heat, cook the bacon for 5 to 7 minutes, or until it's reached preferred doneness.

2. **Butter the bread.** Spread a thin layer of butter on one side of each slice of bread.

3. **Assemble the sandwiches.** With the buttered side down on a plate, top 2 of the slices of bread with 3 slices of Brie and 2 slices of bacon each. For the sandwich tops, spread the unbuttered side of each remaining slice of bread with 1 tablespoon of raspberry jam, and place on top of the bacon buttered-side up.

4. **Prepare the skillet.** Heat a large skillet big enough for both sandwiches over medium heat.

5. **Cook the sandwiches.** Place the sandwiches in the skillet, pressing down with the back of a spatula. Cook for 4 to 5 minutes, until golden brown. Flip, and cook another 4 to 5 minutes. Plate them, then serve and enjoy.

TIP: While I like butter more than most people, I go easy on it here because of the fat content in the bacon and Brie. A thin layer of butter on the bread prior to grilling will do just fine. You can also make these in a panini press if you have one.

SWAP: Use apricot jam or slices of a ripe pear instead of raspberry jam.

Per serving: Calories: 633; Total fat: 34g; Total carbs: 50g; Sugar: 11g; Protein: 31g; Fiber: 2g; Sodium: 1602mg

BLT with Basil Mayonnaise

A BLT with fresh sweet corn is my absolute favorite summer meal. I like to switch things up a little by making it with fresh basil mayonnaise—it's practically summer in a sandwich.

SUPER QUICK

PREP TIME: 10 minutes
COOK TIME: 10 minutes
SERVES: 2

6 slices bacon

⅓ cup mayonnaise

2 tablespoons minced fresh basil

1 scallion, roughly chopped

¼ teaspoon salt

4 slices bread

1 tomato, sliced

2 iceberg lettuce leaves

1. **Cook the bacon.** In a large skillet over medium-high heat, cook the bacon for 5 to 7 minutes, or until it's at your desired crispness. Once the bacon is done, remove it from the pan and place it on a paper towel–lined plate.

2. **Make the basil mayonnaise.** Add the mayonnaise, basil, scallion, and salt to a small food processor and pulse until puréed.

3. **Assemble the sandwiches.** Toast the bread. Spread about 2 tablespoons of the basil mayonnaise on 2 slices of bread. Top each slice with 3 slices of bacon, 2 slices of tomato, 1 lettuce leaf, and one of the remaining slices of toasted bread. Serve and enjoy.

TIP: These BLTs pair well with Summer Vegetable Salad (page 32).

SWAP: Instead of lettuce, use arugula or spinach for some extra leafy-green iron.

Per serving: Calories: 599; Total fat: 39g; Total carbs: 36g; Sugar: 6g; Protein: 26g; Fiber: 2g; Sodium: 2147mg

Thai Curry Noodle Soup

Move over, chicken noodle soup, Thai Curry Noodle Soup is in town and full of flavor! This soup is a breeze to whip up, plus it feels like comfort food while still being bright and cheery.

ONE POT
VEGAN

PREP TIME: 10 minutes
COOK TIME: 15 minutes
SERVES: 2

3 ounces rice noodles

1 tablespoon extra-virgin olive oil

1 red bell pepper, seeded and sliced

½ tablespoon minced fresh ginger

1 garlic clove, minced

1 tablespoon Thai red curry paste

1 (16-ounce) can vegetable broth

1 cup canned coconut milk

2 tablespoons chopped fresh cilantro

1. **Soak the rice noodles.** In a medium bowl, pour 6 cups of very warm water, and add the rice noodles to it.

2. **Cook the red bell pepper.** In a medium pot over medium-high heat, heat the olive oil. Add the bell pepper and cook for 3 to 5 minutes, until slightly softened. Add the ginger, garlic, and Thai red curry paste and cook for 1 minute.

3. **Cook the soup.** Add the vegetable broth, coconut milk, and drained rice noodles, and bring to a boil. Simmer for 5 minutes.

4. **Garnish.** Top with the cilantro. Serve and enjoy.

SWAP: You can use thin rice noodles in this recipe. Simply follow the same rehydration process. Another great swap is using snow peas instead of red bell pepper as they are also sturdy and crunchy.

Per serving: Calories: 475; Total fat: 40g; Total carbs: 26g; Sugar: 8g; Protein: 9g; Fiber: 4g; Sodium: 1140mg

Carrot-Coconut Soup

Soup may not be the first thing you think of when you see a carrot. But this curry flavored soup may just change that. I love how the sweet carrots and coconut milk combine with the unique flavor of curry. Serve this soup with naan or pita crackers for a light dinner.

ONE POT

VEGAN

PREP TIME: 10 minutes
COOK TIME: 20 minutes
SERVES: 2 or 3

2 tablespoons
extra-virgin olive oil

1 small onion, diced

1 tablespoon minced
fresh ginger

2 garlic cloves, minced

4 large carrots,
peeled and chopped
(about 3 cups)

1 (16-ounce) can
coconut milk

1 cup vegetable broth

1 teaspoon curry powder

¼ teaspoon ground
coriander

¼ teaspoon salt

¼ teaspoon freshly
ground black pepper

1. **Cook the vegetables.** In a soup pot over medium-high heat, heat the olive oil. Add the onion, ginger, garlic, and carrots and stir to combine. Cook for about 8 minutes, until the carrots and onion begin to soften.

2. **Cook the soup.** Add the coconut milk, vegetable broth, curry powder, and coriander. Season with the salt and pepper. Bring to a boil and simmer for 10 more minutes.

3. **Serve.** Ladle into bowls. Serve and enjoy.

SWAP: Sweet potatoes are a great swap for carrots as they are similar in consistency, sweetness, and cooking time. Peel 1 large sweet potato and cut into small dice. Cook according to the recipe.

Per serving: Calories: 754; Total fat: 69g; Total carbs: 34g; Sugar: 17g; Protein: 10g; Fiber: 10g; Sodium: 809mg

Chipotle Lentil Soup

Lentils are one of my go-to sources of vegetarian protein. I like both red and green lentils, but I use red lentils in this recipe as they cook much faster. The sauce from the canned chipotles in adobo gives this soup a kick, and I like topping it with a dollop of sour cream or Greek yogurt to cool it down a bit.

ONE POT
VEGAN

PREP TIME: 10 minutes
COOK TIME: 20 minutes
SERVES: 2 or 3

1 tablespoon extra-virgin olive oil

½ small white onion diced

1 large carrot, diced

1 celery stalk, diced

¼ teaspoon salt

Freshly ground black pepper

1 to 2 teaspoons chipotles in adobo sauce

1 teaspoon cumin

1 (15-ounce) can crushed tomatoes

¾ cup red lentils

2 cups water, plus more if needed

2 tablespoons chopped fresh cilantro

1. **Cook the vegetables.** In a medium stockpot over medium-high heat, heat the olive oil. Add the onion, carrot, and celery. Season with the salt and pepper. Cook, stirring often, for 5 to 7 minutes, until the vegetables begin to soften.

2. **Cook the soup.** Add the chipotles in adobo sauce, cumin, crushed tomatoes, lentils, and water. Bring the soup to a boil and let simmer for 10 minutes, or until the lentils are softened. Add more water if you would like a thinner consistency.

3. **Garnish.** Top with the cilantro. Serve and enjoy.

TIP: Another recipe in this cookbook that uses half of an onion is One-Skillet Shepherd's Pie (page 122). So you can go ahead and chop the entire onion, but freeze half of it (for up to a week) to use in that recipe.

SWAP: If you aren't keen on lentils, try a can of pinto beans instead. Since the beans are cooked, you'll cut back the cooking time by 5 minutes.

Per serving: Calories: 426; Total fat: 8g; Total carbs: 66g; Sugar: 16g; Protein: 24g; Fiber: 30g; Sodium: 738mg

Sausage and Tortellini Soup

This is one of those soups that tastes like it takes a lot of work, but it doesn't. A jar of great marinara is the key, so be sure to use your favorite. Top it with a sprinkle of Parmesan cheese and serve with some garlic bread for a complete meal.

ONE POT

PREP TIME: 10 minutes
COOK TIME: 15 minutes
SERVES: 2 or 3

1 tablespoon extra-virgin olive oil

½ small onion, diced

½ pound Italian sausage

1 (24-ounce) jar marinara

1 (16-ounce) can chicken broth

8 ounces refrigerated cheese tortellini

2 cups baby spinach

½ cup heavy cream

½ cup grated Parmesan cheese, divided

1. **Cook the onion and sausage.** In a soup pot over medium-high heat, heat the olive oil. Add the onion and sausage. Cook for 5 to 7 minutes, or until the onion is soft and the sausage is cooked through. Be sure to break up the sausage with a wooden spoon as you go.

2. **Cook the tortellini.** Add the marinara, chicken broth, and tortellini to the same pot. Cook for another 5 minutes, or until the tortellini is cooked through. Add the spinach, heavy cream, and ¼ cup of Parmesan, and stir, cooking 1 more minute until the spinach is wilted.

3. **Garnish.** Top with the remaining ¼ cup of Parmesan cheese. Serve and enjoy.

TIP: This usually makes enough for two, plus one serving left over for lunch the next day. The tortellini often soaks up the remaining broth, so when reheating the leftovers, add a couple of tablespoons of water.

SWAP: If you want to lower the fat content in this soup, use Italian chicken sausage instead of traditional Italian pork sausage.

Per serving: Calories: 1268; Total fat: 86g; Total carbs: 76g; Sugar: 20g; Protein: 52g; Fiber: 10g; Sodium: 3215mg

Southwestern Turkey Chili

Some chili recipes call for the ingredients to be cooked for hours, but that isn't necessary with this easy recipe. I use salsa to add flavor and bulk up the chili. I like to serve this topped with cheddar cheese, along with tortilla chips.

ONE POT
SUPER QUICK

PREP TIME: 5 minutes
COOK TIME: 15 minutes
SERVES: 2 or 3

1 tablespoon extra-virgin olive oil

1 small red onion, chopped

8 ounces lean ground turkey

1 (15-ounce) can black beans, drained and rinsed

1 cup frozen corn

1 (16-ounce) jar salsa

½ tablespoon chili powder

1 teaspoon cumin

½ cup water

¼ teaspoon salt

¼ teaspoon freshly ground black pepper

Shredded cheddar cheese, for topping

1. **Cook the turkey and onion.** In a medium pot over medium-high heat, heat the olive oil. Add the onion and turkey. Cook for 5 to 7 minutes, or until the onion is softened and the turkey is cooked through.

2. **Add the remaining ingredients.** Add the black beans, corn, salsa, chili powder, cumin, and water. Season with the salt and pepper.

3. **Simmer.** Reduce heat and simmer for 5 minutes.

4. **Garnish.** Top with shredded cheese. Serve and enjoy.

TIP: Most prepackaged ground meat is sold by the pound, so if you can, buy your ground meat from the butcher counter to get the exact amount you need. If that isn't an option for you, divide the meat into 4- or 8-ounce servings and freeze what you don't use right away.

SWAP: You can use ground beef or chicken in place of turkey. While chicken and turkey may be lower in fat, ground beef is a great source of iron and increases the richness of the chili.

Per serving: Calories: 635; Total fat: 23g; Total carbs: 70g; Sugar: 10g; Protein: 45g; Fiber: 22g; Sodium: 1892mg

Cold Soba Noodle Vegetable Bowls, *page 52*

CHAPTER FOUR

VEGETABLE MAINS

Eat your vegetables! That phrase we all heard as children is still true for us as adults. But many people don't know how to do that beyond simple salads. Adding more vegetables into your diet is easy. For starters, vegetables are truly versatile; there are countless ways to build meals around them. Plus, replacing a meat-based meal with a vegetable-based one brings many health benefits. And with vegetarian mains like Black Bean and Goat Cheese Tacos (page 54), Thai Peanut Noodles (page 51), and Brown Butter Brussels Sprouts Spaghetti (page 63), they'll also be tasty.

Carrot and Leek Fritters with Dill Dipping Sauce

Fritters are a great way to get a serving of vegetables. In this recipe I shred the carrots and finely chop the leeks to get the most flavor from each vegetable. The yogurt dill dipping sauce perfectly complements the spring vegetables. Serve the fritters warm, and with a simple side salad for a complete meal.

VEGETARIAN

PREP TIME: 10 minutes
COOK TIME: 20 minutes
SERVES: 2

1 large leek, sliced and finely chopped

3 to 4 large carrots, shredded (about 4 cups)

¼ cup all-purpose or whole-wheat flour

3 eggs, whisked

½ cup crumbled goat cheese

¼ teaspoon salt, plus more for the sauce

Pinch freshly ground black pepper, plus more for the sauce

3 tablespoons extra-virgin olive oil

½ cup plain Greek yogurt

2 tablespoons chopped fresh dill

1. **Prepare the fritters.** In a medium bowl, place the leek, carrots, flour, eggs, and goat cheese, and stir to combine. Season with ¼ teaspoon of salt and a pinch of pepper.

2. **Cook the fritters.** In a large skillet over medium-high heat, heat the olive oil. Form the carrot and leek mixture into patties, about the same circumference as a ½-cup measuring cup. You should have 6 fritters total. Place the fritters, two or three at a time, in the large skillet, flattening them with the back of a spatula. Initially, these may seem like they aren't going to stick together, but they will bind up while cooking in the skillet. Cook for 4 to 5 minutes on each side, until golden brown and warmed through.

3. **Make the yogurt sauce.** In a medium bowl, mix the yogurt and dill, and season with salt and pepper.

4. **Garnish.** Top the fritters with yogurt sauce. Serve and enjoy.

SWAP: You can use sour cream in place of the Greek yogurt and feta cheese instead of goat cheese. Basil, thyme, or even parsley will also make a good substitute if you don't have any dill on hand.

Per serving: Calories: 471; Total fat: 30g; Total carbs: 33g; Sugar: 10g; Protein: 19g; Fiber: 4g; Sodium: 527mg

Grilled Vegetable Platter with Chipotle-Yogurt Dipping Sauce

This vegetable platter is great for a lighter main dish or as a fun summer appetizer. If you want to round the meal out, brush some olive oil on fresh bread and grill it for 1 minute on each side, then serve it with the vegetable platter.

VEGETARIAN

PREP TIME: 10 minutes
COOK TIME: 15 minutes
SERVES: 2

8 ounces whole mushrooms

1 red bell pepper, seeded and cut into 2-inch pieces

1 small zucchini, cut into ½-inch slices

1 red onion, cut into 2-inch pieces

2 tablespoons extra-virgin olive oil

1 teaspoon cumin, divided

2 teaspoons chipotles in adobo sauce, divided

¼ teaspoon salt, plus more for the sauce

¼ teaspoon freshly ground black pepper, plus more for the sauce

¾ cup plain Greek yogurt

1 tablespoon freshly squeezed lime juice

1. **Prepare the grill.** Preheat the grill to medium-high heat.

2. **Prepare the vegetables.** In a medium bowl, toss the mushrooms, bell pepper, zucchini, and onion with the olive oil, ½ teaspoon of cumin, and 1 teaspoon of chipotles in adobo sauce. Season with the salt and pepper.

3. **Grill the vegetables.** Place the vegetables on a grill pan, and grill for 10 to 15 minutes, until lightly charred and cooked.

4. **Prepare the chipotle yogurt sauce.** Combine the Greek yogurt, lime juice, remaining ½ teaspoon of cumin, and remaining 1 teaspoon of chipotles in adobo sauce and stir well to combine. Season with salt and pepper.

5. **Serve.** Serve the grilled vegetables with the yogurt sauce on the side and enjoy.

TIP: Purée the rest of the can of chipotles in adobo sauce and freeze it in a plastic baggie. Then the next time you need some, just chop off a piece from the frozen chunk.

SWAP: Summer squash, white onions, or any kind of bell pepper can be used in this recipe.

Per serving: Calories: 299; Total fat: 16g; Total carbs: 19g; Sugar: 12g; Protein: 25g; Fiber: 3g; Sodium: 391mg

Thai Peanut Noodles

These Thai Peanut Noodles are big on flavor but low on effort. The peanut sauce is a breeze to whip up, and I use frozen stir-fry vegetables, which means no chopping. If you like things on the spicier side, add a little more of the chili garlic sauce.

VEGETARIAN

PREP TIME: 10 minutes
COOK TIME: 20 minutes
SERVES: 2 or 3

5 to 6 ounces whole-wheat spaghetti

¼ cup natural creamy peanut butter

2 tablespoons soy sauce

½ tablespoon chili garlic sauce

½ tablespoon honey

1 teaspoon minced fresh ginger

1 tablespoon freshly squeezed lime juice

¼ cup water

1 tablespoon extra-virgin olive oil

2 cups frozen stir-fry vegetables

1. **Cook the spaghetti.** In a large pot of water, cook the whole-wheat spaghetti according to package instructions.

2. **Make the peanut sauce.** While the pasta is cooking, make the sauce. In a food processor, combine the peanut butter, soy sauce, chili garlic sauce, honey, ginger, lime juice, and water, and blend. Set aside.

3. **Cook the vegetables.** In a large skillet over medium-high heat, heat the olive oil. Add the vegetables and cook until warmed through, about 5 minutes.

4. **Assemble.** Add the cooked spaghetti to the skillet along with the peanut sauce, and toss to combine. Serve and enjoy.

TIP: I prefer using natural peanut butter, which doesn't contain any added sugar.

SWAP: You can use almond butter in place of peanut butter for a subtler flavor.

Per serving: Calories: 574; Total fat: 24g; Total carbs: 74g; Sugar: 10g; Protein: 23g; Fiber: 5g; Sodium: 928mg

Cold Soba Noodle Vegetable Bowls

Soba noodles are perfect for weeknight meals because of their quick cook time—usually just 5 to 7 minutes. They're also a good gluten-free option because the noodles are made from buckwheat flour.

SUPER QUICK
VEGAN

PREP TIME: 10 minutes
COOK TIME: 10 minutes
SERVES: 2

4 ounces soba noodles

¼ cup almond butter

1½ tablespoons
soy sauce

1 tablespoon sesame oil

1 teaspoon agave syrup

1 teaspoon minced
fresh ginger

2 garlic cloves, minced

½ cup shredded carrots

1 cup snow peas,
julienned

1. **Cook the soba noodles.** Bring a medium pot of water to a boil. Add the soba noodles and cook according to package instructions. Once they are done cooking, place the noodles in a bowl of cold water and swish around with your hands. Drain and set aside.

2. **Make the sauce.** In a small bowl, combine the almond butter, soy sauce, sesame oil, agave, ginger, and garlic, and stir to combine.

3. **Assemble.** Add the soba noodles to the sauce with the carrots and snow peas and toss to combine. Serve cold and enjoy.

TIP: Soba noodles can get mushy if they cook too long or maintain their excess starch after cooking, so it's important not to skip the step of swishing the noodles around in cold water.

SWAP: Freshly diced zucchini in place of snow peas also works well in this recipe.

Per serving: Calories: 542; Total fat: 26g; Total carbs: 68g; Sugar: 14g; Protein: 17g; Fiber: 5g; Sodium: 1292mg

Tropical Quinoa Bowls with Avocado Dressing

Grain bowls have become extremely popular over the past few years, and with good reason. They're healthy and delicious. I'm always looking for different ways to jazz up my bowl dishes, but this tropical quinoa never gets old.

VEGETARIAN

PREP TIME: 15 minutes
COOK TIME: 15 minutes
SERVES: 2

½ cup quinoa

1 cup water

1 fresh mango

1 red bell pepper

½ ripe avocado, peeled and pitted

2 tablespoons freshly squeezed lime juice

2 tablespoons extra-virgin olive oil

4 tablespoons chopped fresh cilantro, divided

1 tablespoon honey

Salt

Freshly ground black pepper

1 (15-ounce) can chickpeas, drained and rinsed

1. **Cook the quinoa.** In a small pot over high heat, mix together the quinoa and water, and bring to a boil. Reduce heat, cover, and simmer for 15 minutes, until the quinoa is cooked.

2. **Prep the mango and bell pepper.** For the mango, peel the skin off with a vegetable peeler. Cut the flesh to the pit lengthwise and then crosswise. Slice the flesh from the pit, then dice the mango into bite-size pieces. Stem, seed, and dice the bell pepper.

3. **Make the dressing.** In a food processor, blend the avocado, lime juice, olive oil, 2 tablespoons of cilantro, and honey. Season with salt and pepper.

4. **Assemble.** Put ½ cup of quinoa in each of two bowls and evenly divide the mango, chickpeas, bell pepper, and remaining 2 tablespoons of cilantro between the bowls.

5. **Drizzle.** Drizzle the bowls with the avocado dressing. Serve and enjoy.

TIP: To speed up the process, cook the quinoa while you chop the mango and bell pepper and make the sauce.

SWAP: Brown or white rice, bulgur, wheat berries, and couscous are excellent substitutions for the quinoa. You can also use black beans instead of chickpeas, and pineapple instead of mango.

Per serving: Calories: 792; Total fat: 27g; Total carbs: 125g; Sugar: 35g; Protein: 21g; Fiber: 20g; Sodium: 806mg

Black Bean and Goat Cheese Tacos

One of the advantages of making a vegetarian meal is how quickly it comes together since you don't have to wait for meat to be cooked. These black bean and goat cheese tacos are the perfect example. Taco Tuesday has never been so delicious.

SUPER QUICK

VEGETARIAN

PREP TIME: 10 minutes
COOK TIME: 10 minutes
SERVES: 2

1 tablespoon extra-virgin olive oil

1 (15-ounce) can black beans, drained and rinsed

½ teaspoon cumin

1 teaspoon chili powder

½ teaspoon garlic powder

¼ teaspoon salt

4 taco-size corn or flour tortillas

½ cup crumbled goat cheese

½ avocado, peeled, pitted, and sliced

1. **Season and warm the black beans.** In a medium saucepan over medium-high heat, heat the olive oil. Add the black beans, cumin, chili powder, garlic powder, and salt. Stir well to combine. Heat for 5 minutes, letting the beans get warm.

2. **Warm the tortillas.** Place the tortillas on a microwave-safe plate and cover with a damp paper towel. Microwave for 30 to 45 seconds, until warm.

3. **Assemble the tacos.** Divide the beans among the tortillas and top with the goat cheese and avocado. Serve and enjoy.

SWAP: Instead of goat cheese, use a similarly salty crumbled cheese, such as feta.

Per serving: Calories: 492; Total fat: 18g; Total carbs: 68g; Sugar: 1g; Protein: 21g; Fiber: 22g; Sodium: 352mg

Mexican Vegetable Quinoa Skillet

This hearty but healthy dish takes minimal work and only one pot. Since the majority of the flavor in this dish comes from the salsa, make sure you buy one that is made from high-quality ingredients. I prefer using refrigerated salsas.

ONE POT
VEGETARIAN

PREP TIME: 10 minutes
COOK TIME: 20 minutes
SERVES: 2 or 3

1 cup frozen corn

1 cup canned black beans, drained and rinsed

1 cup salsa

¾ cup quinoa

1½ cups water

1 cup shredded cheddar cheese

2 tablespoons chopped fresh cilantro

1 small tomato, diced

½ avocado, peeled, pitted, and sliced

1. **Combine the ingredients.** In an 8- or 9-inch cast-iron skillet over medium-high heat, combine the corn, black beans, salsa, quinoa, and water.

2. **Cook the quinoa.** Bring the mixture to a boil, reduce heat, cover, and simmer for 15 to 18 minutes, until the quinoa is cooked through.

3. **Add the cheese.** Top with the cheddar cheese and cover for another 1 to 2 minutes, until the cheese is melted.

4. **Top it off.** Top with the cilantro, diced tomato, and avocado. Serve and enjoy.

TIP: Avocado is a great source of healthy fat, so use the other half the next morning to top your eggs.

SWAP: Top with a shredded Mexican cheese blend instead of cheddar cheese for a subtler flavor.

Per serving: Calories: 668; Total fat: 30g; Total carbs: 75g; Sugar: 7g; Protein: 31g; Fiber: 15g; Sodium: 1168mg

Vegetarian Enchiladas with Avocado Sauce

Enchiladas are great for a crowd, but a huge pan of them is hard for one or two people to finish, so I've scaled down one of my favorite enchilada recipes. The avocado in the sauce isn't traditional, but it lends a bit of thickness and depth to the dish.

VEGETARIAN

PREP TIME: 15 minutes
COOK TIME: 15 minutes
SERVES: 2

¾ cup water

½ cup sour cream

1 avocado, peeled and pitted

1 (4-ounce) can diced green chiles

1 teaspoon cumin

¼ cup chopped fresh cilantro, plus more for garnish

¼ teaspoon salt

1 cup canned black beans, drained and rinsed

6 fajita-size flour tortillas

1½ cups shredded Mexican cheese blend, divided

1. **Prepare.** Preheat the oven to 375°F.

2. **Make the avocado sauce.** In a blender, add the water, sour cream, avocado, green chiles, cumin, cilantro, and salt, and purée. Spread about ½ cup of the sauce on the bottom of a greased 8-by-8-inch baking dish.

3. **Assemble the enchiladas.** Combine ½ cup of the sauce with the black beans. Fill each tortilla with about 2 tablespoons of black beans and 2 tablespoons of cheese. Roll the tortillas and place them, seam-side down, in the prepared baking dish. Top the enchiladas with the remaining sauce and the remaining shredded cheese.

4. **Bake the enchiladas.** Bake in the preheated oven for 15 minutes.

5. **Garnish.** Top with additional chopped cilantro. Serve and enjoy.

TIP: If you have some roasted veggies (or grilled veggies from the Grilled Vegetable Platter with Chipotle-Yogurt Dipping Sauce, page 50) in the refrigerator that need to be used up, toss them in the filling with the beans.

SWAP: If you like your enchiladas spicy, used canned jalapeños instead of green chiles. You can also use plain whole-milk Greek yogurt in place of sour cream to cut some of the calories.

Per serving: Calories: 697; Total fat: 37g; Total carbs: 72g; Sugar: 4g; Protein: 22g; Fiber: 15g; Sodium: 1286mg

Chipotle Chickpea Tacos with Creamy Lime Slaw

These spicy chipotle chickpea tacos are a super fast and satisfying meal that I love to serve on Taco Tuesdays. The heat from the chipotle peppers is countered by a creamy coleslaw for a simple but delicious meal.

SUPER QUICK

VEGETARIAN

PREP TIME: 10 minutes
COOK TIME: 10 minutes
SERVES: 2

1 tablespoon extra-virgin olive oil

1 (16-ounce) can chickpeas, drained and rinsed

1 to 2 tablespoons chipotles in adobo sauce, depending on your spice tolerance

½ teaspoon cumin

1 cup shredded red cabbage

1 tablespoon freshly squeezed lime juice

2 tablespoons mayonnaise

2 tablespoons chopped fresh cilantro

Salt

Freshly ground black pepper

4 taco-size flour tortillas

1. **Heat the oil.** In a medium skillet over medium-high heat, heat the olive oil.

2. **Cook the chickpeas.** Add the chickpeas, chipotles in adobo sauce, and cumin, stirring to combine. Cook for 5 to 7 minutes, until the chickpeas start to get crispy.

3. **Prepare the slaw.** Put the cabbage in a medium bowl. Add the lime juice, mayonnaise, and cilantro and stir to combine. Season with salt and pepper.

4. **Warm the tortillas.** Place the tortillas on a microwave-safe plate and cover with a damp paper towel. Microwave for 30 to 45 seconds, until warm.

5. **Assemble the tacos.** Spoon the chickpeas into the tortillas and top with slaw. Serve and enjoy.

TIP: To save time, use preshredded cabbage. You can find it in the refrigerated produce section in most grocery stores.

SWAP: You can use any kind of beans in this recipe. To make this dish gluten-free, use corn tortillas instead of flour tortillas.

Per serving: Calories: 519; Total fat: 16g; Total carbs: 82g; Sugar: 3g; Protein: 15g; Fiber: 15g; Sodium: 851mg

Cauliflower-Chickpea Curry

Anyone who thinks vegan food can't be hearty and comforting needs to come to my house for a bowl of my Cauliflower-Chickpea Curry. This is comfort food, without a doubt. If you've never made curry, there's no need to be intimidated. This recipe is relatively mild as far as heat, so if you like your curry spicy, add cayenne pepper to your liking.

VEGAN

PREP TIME: 10 minutes
COOK TIME: 20 minutes
SERVES: 2 or 3

1 tablespoon coconut oil

1 small white onion, diced

2 garlic cloves, minced

3 cups (about half a head) cauliflower florets, chopped

¼ teaspoon salt

Pinch freshly ground black pepper

1 (16-ounce) can chickpeas, drained and rinsed

1 cup frozen peas

2 teaspoons curry powder

1 teaspoon garam masala

1 (16-ounce) can coconut milk

1. **Cook the vegetables.** In a large saucepan over medium-high heat, heat the coconut oil. Add the onion, garlic, and cauliflower. Season with the salt and pepper, and cook for 10 minutes, until the onion and cauliflower are softened.

2. **Add the remaining ingredients.** Add the chickpeas, peas, curry powder, garam masala, and coconut milk, stirring well to combine. Cook for another 5 to 10 minutes, until the vegetables are all tender and warm.

3. **Serve.** Serve over rice or quinoa, as desired.

TIP: I often buy bagged fresh or frozen cauliflower to save on prep time and cleanup time. You will likely have one serving of leftovers after this meal, which is great because curry always tastes better the next day.

SWAP: The coconut oil used here pairs nicely with the curry powder. But if you don't have any on hand, go ahead and use olive oil in its place.

Per serving: Calories: 958; Total fat: 64g; Total carbs: 86g; Sugar: 15g; Protein: 23g; Fiber: 23g; Sodium: 1160mg

Red Lentil Curry

Lentils are an excellent source of protein when cooking vegetarian meals. I serve this curry with a side of naan, which is a fluffy Indian bread that is perfectly shaped for getting the last bit from your bowl.

SUPER QUICK
VEGAN

PREP TIME: 5 minutes
COOK TIME: 15 minutes
SERVES: 2

⅓ cup white rice

3 cups water

¾ cup red lentils

½ cup coconut milk

1 tablespoon curry powder

½ teaspoon turmeric

1 teaspoon cumin

½ teaspoon salt

Juice of 1 lime

¼ cup chopped fresh cilantro

1. **Cook the rice.** In a small pot over medium-high heat, cook the rice according to package instructions.

2. **Cook the lentils.** Meanwhile, in a medium pot over high heat, bring the water to a boil. Add the lentils and cook until soft, stirring often, about 10 minutes. Drain the lentils if needed and return them to the pot. Add the coconut milk, curry powder, turmeric, cumin, salt, and lime juice. Stir well to combine.

3. **Assemble.** Top the rice with the lentils and cilantro. Serve and enjoy.

TIP: You can use brown or green lentils in the dish, but I prefer red lentils since they cook much faster. If you use brown or green, add 10 minutes to the cooking time.

SWAP: To reduce the amount of carbohydrates in this dish, serve with quinoa instead of white rice.

Per serving: Calories: 521; Total fat: 16g; Total carbs: 74g; Sugar: 4g; Protein: 23g; Fiber: 24g; Sodium: 601mg

Parmesan Spinach Gnocchi

I fell in love with gnocchi while working in an Italian restaurant during graduate school. The fluffy little potato pillows are irresistible to me. I rarely go through the work of making my own gnocchi; the ones you can buy at the store are so easy to cook. If you've never made your own cream sauce, don't be afraid—it really is very easy. This one gets a boost of flavor from the addition of fresh basil and lemon zest.

SUPER QUICK
VEGETARIAN

PREP TIME: 10 minutes
COOK TIME: 10 minutes
SERVES: 2

8 ounces potato gnocchi

1 tablespoon butter

1 garlic clove, minced

1 tablespoon flour

¾ cup whole milk

1 cup chopped
fresh spinach

2 tablespoons chopped
fresh basil

Zest of ½ lemon

¾ cup shredded
Parmesan cheese

Salt

Freshly ground
black pepper

1. **Cook the gnocchi.** Bring a medium pot of water to a boil. Add the gnocchi and cook until it floats to the top. Drain and set aside.

2. **Make the Parmesan cream sauce.** As the gnocchi cooks, in a medium saucepan over medium heat, melt the butter. Once the butter is melted, add the garlic and cook for 1 minute. Add the flour and stir well to incorporate. Slowly add the milk, whisking continuously, to create a cream sauce. Add the spinach, basil, lemon zest, and Parmesan cheese, and whisk until the Parmesan cheese is melted.

3. **Assemble.** When the gnocchi is cooked, drain the pasta, then add it to the cream sauce. Toss to combine. Season with salt and pepper. Serve and enjoy.

SWAP: You can use any kind of pasta in place of gnocchi, such as penne or macaroni. In that case, just cook it according to package instructions.

Per serving: Calories: 551; Total fat: 19g; Total carbs: 69g; Sugar: 7g; Protein: 27g; Fiber: 5g; Sodium: 1200mg

Pumpkin Fettuccine Alfredo

When autumn rolls around and there's a chill in the air, I start craving all things pumpkin. Not just sweet pumpkin treats, but savory pumpkin dishes, including this Pumpkin Fettuccine Alfredo. The sauce can be made with milk or heavy cream, depending on what you have on hand and how rich you want it to be.

VEGETARIAN

PREP TIME: 10 minutes
COOK TIME: 20 minutes
SERVES: 2

6 ounces fettuccine or linguine

1 tablespoon butter

1 small shallot, diced

1 garlic clove, minced

¼ teaspoon salt, divided, plus more for seasoning

1 tablespoon flour

1½ cups whole milk

1 cup canned pumpkin purée

⅛ teaspoon cinnamon

⅛ teaspoon nutmeg

½ cup grated Parmesan cheese, divided

1. **Cook the fettuccine.** Bring a medium pot of water to a boil. Add the pasta and cook according to package instructions. Drain and set aside.

2. **Start the pumpkin alfredo sauce.** In the meantime, in a medium skillet over medium heat, melt the butter. Add the shallot and garlic, and cook for 5 minutes, until softened. Season with ⅛ teaspoon of salt. Add the flour, mixing to combine, and cook for 1 minute.

3. **Add the milk.** Very slowly pour in the milk, whisking vigorously to incorporate. Bring the mixture back to a simmer.

4. **Add the remaining ingredients.** Whisk in the pumpkin purée, cinnamon, nutmeg, remaining ⅛ teaspoon of salt, and ¼ cup of Parmesan cheese, until the cheese is melted. Cook for 2 to 3 more minutes.

5. **Assemble the pasta.** Add the cooked pasta to the skillet and toss with the sauce. Season with additional salt, to preference.

6. **Garnish.** Top with the remaining ¼ cup of Parmesan cheese and enjoy.

TIP: If you have any fresh sage on hand, chop up about a tablespoon of it, and toss it in at the end for an extra fragrant flavor.

SWAP: You can use 1 percent milk instead of whole milk.

Per serving: Calories: 724; Total fat: 20g; Total carbs: 121g; Sugar: 13g; Protein: 29g; Fiber: 32g; Sodium: 676mg

Creamy Sun-Dried Tomato Pesto Pasta

Pesto isn't only for basil. A jar of sun-dried tomatoes also makes a tasty sauce, especially if you can find the kind with Italian herbs. This pesto is great with any type of pasta, but my favorite is penne.

VEGETARIAN

PREP TIME: 10 minutes
COOK TIME: 15 minutes
SERVES: 2

6 to 8 ounces
penne pasta

½ cup jarred sun-dried
tomatoes in Italian herbs
and olive oil

2 garlic cloves

2 tablespoons pine nuts

¼ cup extra-virgin
olive oil

Salt

Freshly ground
black pepper

4 ounces cream cheese

½ cup heavy cream

½ cup shredded
Parmesan cheese

1. **Cook the pasta.** Bring a medium pot of water to a boil. Add the pasta and cook according to package instructions. Drain and set aside.

2. **Make the sun-dried tomato pesto.** As the pasta cooks, in a small food processor, combine the sun-dried tomatoes, garlic, and pine nuts. Pulse the mixture until a paste forms. Add the olive oil and pulse until everything is well combined. Season with salt and pepper.

3. **Assemble the pasta.** In a large skillet over medium heat, mix the pesto, cream cheese, and heavy cream. Stir well to incorporate. Let the sauce cook for 2 to 3 minutes, until it is slightly thickened. Add the cooked pasta to the skillet and combine.

4. **Garnish.** Top with the Parmesan cheese. Serve and enjoy.

TIP: If you can't find herbed sun-dried tomatoes, throw in a pinch dried basil, thyme, and parsley when blending.

SWAP: Pine nuts can be quite costly, so a more affordable option is to use walnuts instead.

Per serving: Calories: 989; Total fat: 81g; Total carbs: 50g; Sugar: 3g; Protein: 23g; Fiber: 3g; Sodium: 454mg

Brown Butter Brussels Sprouts Spaghetti

I am a firm believer that brown butter makes anything and everything taste better— from cookies and brownies to pasta and vegetables. This Brussels sprouts spaghetti is no exception.

5-INGREDIENT

VEGETARIAN

PREP TIME: 10 minutes
COOK TIME: 20 minutes
SERVES: 2

4 ounces spaghetti

4 tablespoons unsalted butter

2 tablespoons extra-virgin olive oil

1½ cups Brussels sprouts, finely chopped

½ cup shredded Parmesan cheese

¼ teaspoon salt

Pinch freshly ground black pepper

1. **Cook the pasta.** Bring a medium pot of water to a boil. Add the pasta and cook according to package instructions. Drain the water when done but keep the pasta in the pot for assembly.

2. **Brown the butter.** While the pasta cooks, brown the butter in a small saucepan over medium-low heat. Cook the butter over medium-low heat until the butter turns golden brown, 7 to 10 minutes. Try not to stir the butter, just swirl the pan. Once the butter has browned, pour it into a bowl.

3. **Cook the Brussels sprouts.** In a medium saucepan, add the olive oil and Brussels sprouts. Cook over medium-high heat for 7 to 10 minutes, until softened and cooked.

4. **Assemble.** In the pot with the drained pasta, add the browned butter, Brussels sprouts, and ¼ cup of Parmesan cheese. Toss to combine. Season with the salt and pepper.

5. **Garnish.** Top with the remaining ¼ cup of Parmesan cheese. Serve and enjoy.

SWAP: Penne pasta also works in this recipe. It makes a sturdy pairing with the hearty, fibrous Brussels sprouts (as opposed to a more delicate pasta, like orzo or angel hair).

Per serving: Calories: 654; Total fat: 44g; Total carbs: 50g; Sugar: 3g; Protein: 19g; Fiber: 4g; Sodium: 734mg

Roasted Balsamic Portobello Mushroom Burgers with Garlic Fries

Portobello mushrooms are hearty, they won't fall apart when cooked, and they soak up any flavor you put on them. Since I can't have a burger without fries, I included my favorite recipe for oven fries here, too. The trick with timing is to pop them in the oven before you start on the burgers and they'll be done just in time.

VEGETARIAN

PREP TIME: 10 minutes
COOK TIME: 20 minutes
SERVES: 2

Nonstick cooking spray

1 large russet potato, peeled and cut into thin strips

3 tablespoons extra-virgin olive oil, divided

1 teaspoon garlic powder

Salt

Freshly ground black pepper

2 portobello mushrooms, stemmed and washed

1 tablespoon balsamic vinegar, plus more for serving

¼ cup jarred roasted red peppers

½ cup crumbled goat cheese

2 ciabatta buns

1 cup arugula leaves

1. **Prepare.** Preheat the oven to 450°F. Line a baking sheet with aluminum foil and spray with nonstick cooking spray.

2. **Roast the fries.** Place the fries on the prepared baking sheet and drizzle with 1 tablespoon of olive oil. Sprinkle with the garlic powder, season with salt and pepper, and toss to combine. Bake in the preheated oven for 20 minutes.

3. **Prepare the mushrooms.** While the fries are baking, drizzle the portobello mushrooms with the remaining 2 tablespoons of olive oil and the balsamic vinegar, and season with salt and pepper.

4. **Bake the mushrooms.** Place the mushrooms on a baking sheet and cook for 12 minutes, until they are soft. The fries will still be in the oven at this point.

5. **Assemble.** Remove the mushrooms from the oven and top with the roasted red peppers and goat cheese. Place the portobellos on sliced ciabatta buns and top with the arugula. Drizzle with additional balsamic vinegar. When the fries are done, remove them from the oven and serve alongside the burgers.

TIP: These portobello burgers are also great when made on the grill. Place the mushrooms on a grill or in a grill pan, and cook for 12 minutes, watching closely so they don't burn.

SWAP: Use fresh baby spinach instead of arugula. You can also use fresh mozzarella instead of goat cheese.

Per serving: Calories: 379; Total fat: 23g; Total carbs: 39g; Sugar: 3g; Protein: 9g; Fiber: 4g; Sodium: 119mg

Grilled Cilantro-Lime Chicken, *page 81*

CHAPTER FIVE

POULTRY

Poultry is the number one choice for protein consumed in America. In the last decade or so, consumers have figured out that chicken and turkey are healthy and affordable meal options—something countries around the world figured out a while ago. In this chapter I've curated a wide variety of poultry dishes that incorporate easy-to-use cooking techniques and ingredients. With recipes ranging from Coconut Chicken Curry (page 73) to Turkey Parmesan Meatballs with Creamy Tomato Sauce (page 76), I hope you feel like you are traveling the world as you cook your way through!

Asian Chicken Lettuce Wraps

If you think you have to go to a restaurant for delicious lettuce wraps, think again. These chicken lettuce wraps aren't just super quick to make, they're also full of flavor. The water chestnuts add a delightful extra crunch.

ONE POT
SUPER QUICK

PREP TIME: 5 minutes
COOK TIME: 10 minutes
SERVES: 2

1 tablespoon extra-virgin olive oil

8 ounces ground chicken

2 garlic cloves, minced

1 tablespoon soy sauce

2 tablespoons hoisin sauce

1 teaspoon sriracha

1 (8-ounce) can water chestnuts, drained and diced

6 butter lettuce leaves

¼ cup chopped scallions

1. **Cook the chicken.** In a medium skillet over medium-high heat, heat the olive oil. Add the ground chicken, breaking it up into small pieces to ensure it is browned and cooked through, about 5 minutes.

2. **Add the other ingredients.** Add the garlic, and cook for another minute. Add the soy sauce, hoisin sauce, sriracha, and water chestnuts. Cook for another 2 minutes.

3. **Assemble.** Spoon the chicken mixture into the lettuce leaves and top with the scallions. Serve and enjoy.

TIP: Look for hoisin sauce in the Asian section of your grocery store.

SWAP: You can use ground turkey or even beef instead of ground chicken. And if you can't find butter lettuce leaves, iceberg lettuce is a suitable substitute.

Per serving: Calories: 447; Total fat: 17g; Total carbs: 48g; Sugar: 5g; Protein: 24g; Fiber: 1g; Sodium: 813mg

Hawaiian Chicken Sliders

What is it that makes sliders more fun than regular-sized sandwiches? These Hawaiian chicken sliders are sweet, smoky, and cheesy. The sweetness of the barbecue sauce is the perfect contrast to the saltiness of the provolone cheese.

PREP TIME: 15 minutes
COOK TIME: 15 minutes
SERVES: 2

1 boneless skinless chicken breast, cut into two pieces

½ cup barbecue sauce

4 slider buns

4 slices provolone cheese

4 pineapple rings

½ cup shredded red cabbage

1. **Cook and prepare the chicken.** Over high heat, bring a small pot of water to boil. Add the chicken and boil until cooked through, about 10 minutes. Remove the chicken from the pan. In a small bowl, shred the chicken and toss with the barbecue sauce.

2. **Preheat the broiler.** While the chicken is boiling, preheat the broiler.

3. **Assemble the sliders.** Place one fourth of the chicken on each slider bun bottom, and top with a slice of cheese.

4. **Broil.** Place the sliders on a baking sheet and broil for 1 to 2 minutes, until the cheese is golden.

5. **Assemble.** Top each slider with a pineapple slice, shredded cabbage, and bun top. Serve and enjoy.

TIP: Using rotisserie chicken that you find precooked at the grocery store is a great way to save time with this recipe. Alternatively, if you have a little extra time, place the pineapple slices on a hot grill for 2 to 3 minutes per side to give them more flavor and warmth.

SWAP: Use Swiss cheese instead of provolone for a more robust cheese flavor.

Per serving: Calories: 536; Total fat: 17g; Total carbs: 57g; Sugar: 30g; Protein: 38g; Fiber: 3g; Sodium: 1422mg

Barbecue Chicken Pizza Flatbreads

When my family wants a traditional pizza, we get delivery. But when I want to save money and the calories, homemade flatbread pizzas come to the rescue. I make these Barbecue Chicken Pizza Flatbreads when I want to recreate a pizza from one of my favorite restaurants. It amazes me how such simple ingredients combine to create such a delicious pizza.

SUPER QUICK

PREP TIME: 10 minutes
COOK TIME: 10 minutes
SERVES: 2

1 boneless skinless chicken breast

Salt

Freshly ground black pepper

1 tablespoon extra-virgin olive oil

1 small red onion, sliced

½ cup frozen corn

¼ cup barbecue sauce

2 medium naan flatbreads

1 cup shredded Colby Jack cheese

2 tablespoons chopped fresh cilantro

1. **Prepare.** Preheat the oven to 400°F.

2. **Prep the chicken.** Pound the chicken until it is only about ½ inch thick, then season it with salt and pepper.

3. **Cook the chicken.** In a small skillet over medium heat, heat the olive oil. Add the chicken and onion. Cook until the onion is soft and the chicken is cooked all the way through, about 5 minutes on each side. Remove the chicken and onion from the pan, and shred or chop the chicken.

4. **Warm the corn.** While the chicken is cooking, place the corn in a small bowl and microwave on high for 1 minute, or until warm.

5. **Assemble the flatbreads.** Spread 2 to 3 tablespoons of barbecue sauce on each flatbread and top with the chicken, onion slices, corn, and cheese.

6. **Bake.** Bake in the preheated oven for 10 minutes, until the cheese is melted.

7. **Garnish.** Top with the cilantro. Serve and enjoy.

TIP: Just like with the Hawaiian Chicken Sliders (page 70), rotisserie chicken is a great time-saving choice for this recipe.

SWAP: A full-size premade pizza crust works here if you want leftovers for lunch the next day.

Per serving: Calories: 489; Total fat: 17g; Total carbs: 55g; Sugar: 14g; Protein: 30g; Fiber: 3g; Sodium: 1191mg

Teriyaki Chicken Rice Bowls

Forget about getting takeout. These bowls will be ready way before the delivery guy would have shown up at your door. The chicken breasts are cooked in a sweet and garlicky homemade teriyaki sauce (made with pantry ingredients you already have!), and the whole thing is served with white rice and steamed broccoli.

PREP TIME: 10 minutes
COOK TIME: 20 minutes
SERVES: 2

1 cup white rice

2 cups fresh broccoli florets

2 tablespoons brown sugar

¼ cup soy sauce

1 tablespoon apple cider vinegar

2 garlic cloves, minced

½ tablespoon cornstarch

½ pound boneless skinless chicken breast, cut into bite-size pieces

1. **Cook the rice.** In a small pot over medium heat, cook the rice according to package instructions.

2. **Cook the broccoli.** Place the broccoli in a microwave-safe bowl with 1 tablespoon of water and cover with a paper towel. Microwave on high for 3 minutes. If it's not fully cooked, microwave for 1 more minute.

3. **Make the teriyaki sauce.** Meanwhile, in a small bowl, whisk together the brown sugar, soy sauce, apple cider vinegar, garlic, and cornstarch.

4. **Cook the chicken.** In a medium skillet over medium-high heat, combine the chicken and sauce. Cook until the chicken is cooked through, 8 to 10 minutes.

5. **Assemble.** Divide the cooked rice between two bowls. Top with the cooked chicken and steamed broccoli. Serve and enjoy.

TIP: Microwaving broccoli is an easy and healthy way to prepare the vegetable, but if you prefer your broccoli a little crispier, you can sauté it in olive oil.

SWAP: You can swap the broccoli for other vegetables that you have on hand, such as snow peas, bell peppers, mushrooms, asparagus, or cauliflower.

Per serving: Calories: 553; Total fat: 2g; Total carbs: 94g; Sugar: 11g; Protein: 37g; Fiber: 4g; Sodium: 1910mg

Coconut Chicken Curry

This curry is pretty mild because my Midwestern taste buds can't handle much heat. If you like things on the spicier side, though, add a bit of cayenne pepper or a jalapeño pepper to kick this dish up. I love serving this curry with steamed rice or rice noodles.

ONE POT

PREP TIME: 10 minutes
COOK TIME: 15 minutes
SERVES: 2 or 3

2 boneless skinless chicken breasts

1 tablespoon coconut oil

1 small onion, chopped

1 garlic clove, minced

1 teaspoon minced fresh ginger

1 tablespoon curry powder

1 tablespoon Thai red curry paste

1 (15-ounce) can coconut milk

½ teaspoon salt

2 tablespoons chopped fresh cilantro

Rice or noodles, for serving

1. **Prep the chicken.** Pound the chicken breasts to even thickness, about 1 inch, and cut into 1-inch pieces.

2. **Cook the chicken and onion.** In a medium skillet over medium-high heat, heat the coconut oil. Add the chicken and onion. Cook until the onion is softened and the chicken is cooked through, 6 to 7 minutes.

3. **Season.** Add the garlic, ginger, curry powder, and curry paste. Cook 1 to 2 more minutes. Add the coconut milk and salt. Bring the mixture to a simmer and let cook for 3 to 4 more minutes.

4. **Assemble.** Serve the chicken curry on top of rice or noodles, sprinkle with the cilantro, and enjoy.

SWAP: If you can't find Thai red curry paste, just add another tablespoon of curry powder.

Per serving: Calories: 727; Total fat: 62g; Total carbs: 20g; Sugar: 9g; Protein: 31g; Fiber: 7g; Sodium: 1082mg

Buffalo Chicken Burritos

These burritos are yet another way to satisfy that craving for spicy chicken wings. Don't worry—I didn't forget about the carrots and celery that are often served alongside Buffalo chicken wings; these burritos have all the essential Buffalo wing components stuffed inside the tortillas for the complete Buffalo chicken experience.

PREP TIME: 10 minutes
COOK TIME: 20 minutes
SERVES: 2

1 tablespoon extra-virgin olive oil

1 large boneless skinless chicken breast, cut into small pieces

½ cup shredded carrots

1 celery stalk, finely chopped

½ cup canned black beans, drained and rinsed

¼ cup Buffalo wing sauce, divided

2 large flour tortillas

¼ cup shredded cheddar cheese

3 tablespoons ranch dressing, divided

1. **Prepare.** Preheat the oven to 400°F.

2. **Cook the chicken.** In a medium skillet over medium-high heat, heat the olive oil. Add the chicken and cook through, about 5 minutes.

3. **Cook the vegetables.** Add the carrots, celery, black beans, and 3 tablespoons of Buffalo wing sauce. Cook for another 5 minutes.

4. **Assemble the burritos.** Place half of the chicken on each tortilla. Top each with 2 tablespoons of cheddar cheese, 1 tablespoon of wing sauce, and 1 tablespoon of ranch dressing. Roll up the burritos, folding in the sides.

5. **Bake.** Place the burritos on a baking sheet, seam-side down, and bake in the preheated oven for 5 minutes.

6. **Top it off.** Top the burritos with the remaining 2 tablespoons of ranch dressing. Serve and enjoy.

TIP: Prep these in advance for easy lunches throughout the week. Assemble the burritos, wrap them in plastic wrap, and refrigerate. If you're in an office or don't have access to an oven, wrap the burrito in a paper towel and microwave for 30 to 60 seconds.

SWAP: Use ground turkey in place of the chicken.

Per serving: Calories: 471; Total fat: 28g; Total carbs: 26g; Sugar: 3g; Protein: 29g; Fiber: 6g; Sodium: 1211mg

One-Pot Chicken Broccoli Alfredo Pasta

Once you make your own alfredo sauce, it's hard to go back to buying the premade jarred sauce. Not only does it taste better, but it's also made with ingredients that you can pronounce. This chicken broccoli alfredo is rich and indulgent, but I've kept the recipe simple enough to prepare for a weeknight meal.

ONE POT

PREP TIME: 10 minutes
COOK TIME: 15 minutes
SERVES: 2 or 3

1 tablespoon extra-virgin olive oil

1 boneless skinless chicken breast, cut into bite-size pieces

½ teaspoon garlic powder

6 ounces penne pasta (about 1½ cups)

2 cups chopped fresh broccoli

1¼ cups chicken broth

1 cup milk

¼ cup heavy cream

1 cup grated Parmesan cheese

¼ teaspoon salt

1. **Cook the chicken.** In a medium skillet heat over medium-high heat, heat the olive oil. Add the chicken and cook for 4 to 5 minutes, until browned and almost cooked through.

2. **Cook the pasta.** Add the garlic powder, pasta, broccoli, chicken broth, and milk. Bring to a boil. Reduce the heat and simmer for 8 to 10 minutes, until the pasta is cooked through and the broccoli is tender.

3. **Finish the sauce.** Add the heavy cream and Parmesan cheese, stirring to combine. Season with the salt. Serve and enjoy.

SWAP: Use fresh spinach instead of broccoli. Just stir it in at the end with the cream and Parmesan cheese.

Per serving: Calories: 780; Total fat: 37g; Total carbs: 58g; Sugar: 10g; Protein: 54g; Fiber: 4g; Sodium: 1448mg

Turkey Parmesan Meatballs with Creamy Tomato Sauce

Homemade meatballs don't have to be difficult or time-consuming! These turkey Parmesan meatballs take only 10 minutes to prep. There's no chopping—just dump everything into a bowl, mix it up, and scoop into meatballs. I add heavy cream to the marinara to make this dish extra rich. I love to serve these meatballs over spaghetti with garlic bread.

PREP TIME: 10 minutes
COOK TIME: 20 minutes
SERVES: 2 or 3

4 ounces spaghetti

8 ounces ground turkey

1 egg, lightly beaten

½ cup shredded Parmesan cheese, divided

1 garlic clove, minced

Pinch salt

3 tablespoons Italian bread crumbs

1 cup jarred marinara sauce

¼ cup heavy cream

1. **Prepare.** Preheat the oven to 425°F.

2. **Cook the spaghetti.** Bring a pot of water to boil and cook the spaghetti according to package instructions. Drain and set aside.

3. **Mix the meatballs.** In a medium bowl, mix the ground turkey, egg, ¼ cup of Parmesan cheese, garlic, salt, and Italian bread crumbs.

4. **Form the meatballs.** Using a cookie dough scoop or spoon, roll the mixture into meatballs that are about 1 tablespoon in size. Place them in a cast-iron skillet.

5. **Make the sauce.** In a small bowl, whisk together the marinara and heavy cream, then pour it over the meatballs. Sprinkle with the remaining ¼ cup of Parmesan cheese.

6. **Bake.** Bake the meatballs in the preheated oven for 15 to 20 minutes.

7. **Serve.** Serve over the spaghetti.

TIP: If you don't have a scooper to make the meatballs, go ahead and use your hands. Be sure to coat your hands with a little olive oil first to keep the meat from sticking to your skin.

SWAP: If you follow a low-carb diet, use spiralized zucchini noodles instead of spaghetti. Many stores now carry them in the refrigerated section near the produce, so you don't need to buy a spiralizer.

Per serving: Calories: 653; Total fat: 25g; Total carbs: 58g; Sugar: 6g; Protein: 48g; Fiber: 3g; Sodium: 914mg

One-Skillet Creamy Lemon Chicken

Sometimes the simplest ingredients can create an amazing dish. The lemon juice and zest, shallot, and heavy cream used here make a luscious sauce. Be sure to serve this dish with a loaf of crusty bread—you'll want it to soak up every last bit of the sauce.

ONE POT

PREP TIME: 5 minutes
COOK TIME: 20 minutes
SERVES: 2

1 tablespoon extra-virgin olive oil

2 boneless skinless chicken breasts

Pinch salt

Pinch freshly ground black pepper

2 tablespoons butter

1 shallot, diced

½ cup chicken broth

½ cup heavy cream

Zest and juice of 1 lemon

2 tablespoons chopped fresh parsley

1. **Cook the chicken.** In a medium skillet over medium-high heat, heat the olive oil. Pound the chicken to ½-inch thickness. Season the chicken with salt and pepper. Add the chicken breasts to the skillet and cook through, about 5 minutes on each side. Remove the chicken from the skillet.

2. **Cook the sauce.** Melt the butter in the skillet. Add the shallot and chicken broth, using a spatula to scrape up any bits on the bottom of the pan. Cook over medium-high heat for 5 minutes, or until the sauce is reduced. Stir in the heavy cream, lemon zest, and lemon juice, and bring to a simmer. Reduce the heat and let simmer for 5 minutes.

3. **Assemble.** Return the chicken breasts to the skillet, and spoon the sauce over them.

4. **Garnish.** Top with fresh parsley. Serve and enjoy.

TIP: Once you add in the cream, keep an eye on it to make sure it does not boil. The fat from the cream will curdle and the sauce will no longer be smooth.

SWAP: Pork tenderloin cutlets are an excellent substitution here. The cuts are super thin, so the cooking time is similar to that of the chicken in this recipe.

Per serving: Calories: 502; Total fat: 42g; Total carbs: 3g; Sugar: 0g; Protein: 29g; Fiber: 0g; Sodium: 450mg

Creamy Salsa Verde Chicken Enchilada Skillet

Sometimes I like taking time my time in the kitchen; stirring a pot of risotto or chopping vegetables can be therapeutic. That said, on days when I don't have the extra time, dishes like this enchilada skillet come to the rescue. Instead of stuffing tortillas with the filling and baking the enchiladas, I cut the tortillas into small pieces and combine them with the sauce and filling for a casserole-like dish. It's a great solution to make enchiladas a quick weeknight dinner!

ONE POT
SUPER QUICK

PREP TIME: 5 minutes
COOK TIME: 15 minutes
SERVES: 2 or 3

1 tablespoon extra-virgin olive oil

1 boneless skinless chicken breast, cut into bite-size pieces

1 cup salsa verde

4 ounces cream cheese

½ teaspoon cumin

¼ teaspoon salt

4 corn or flour tortillas, cut into 1-inch pieces

1 cup shredded Mexican cheese blend

2 tablespoons chopped scallions

½ avocado, peeled, pitted, and sliced

1. **Cook the chicken.** In a medium cast-iron skillet over medium-high heat, heat the olive oil. Add the chicken and cook through, 5 to 7 minutes.

2. **Add the remaining ingredients.** Add the salsa verde, cream cheese, and cumin. Stir until the cream cheese is melted. Season with the salt. Add the tortillas, stirring to combine.

3. **Add the cheese.** Top with the cheese and cook for 1 more minute, letting the cheese melt.

4. **Garnish.** Top with the scallions and sliced avocado. Serve and enjoy.

SWAP: Use 8 ounces of ground turkey or chicken instead of chicken breast. You can also use regular red tomato salsa, if you prefer.

Per serving: Calories: 686; Total fat: 48g; Total carbs: 37g; Sugar: 3g; Protein: 33g; Fiber: 10g; Sodium: 1319mg

Italian Chicken and Green Beans Skillet

Isn't it true that bacon makes everything better? I first made this Italian chicken skillet without it, and although it was tasty, I felt it still needed something. So I added bacon and voilà! It turned the dish from good to great.

ONE POT

PREP TIME: 5 minutes
COOK TIME: 25 minutes
SERVES: 2

1 slice bacon, cut into small pieces

2 boneless skinless chicken thighs

¼ teaspoon salt

Pinch freshly ground black pepper

1 teaspoon Italian seasoning

2 garlic cloves, minced

1 (12-ounce) can diced tomatoes

2 cups fresh green beans

1. **Cook the bacon.** In an 8- or 9-inch cast-iron skillet over medium-high heat, cook the bacon until crispy, about 5 minutes. Remove the bacon from the skillet, but leave about 1 tablespoon of the bacon grease.

2. **Prepare the chicken.** Season the chicken thighs with the salt, pepper, and Italian seasoning.

3. **Cook the chicken.** In the same skillet over medium-high heat, add the chicken thighs. Brown the chicken thighs, 2 to 3 minutes on each side. Add the garlic, diced tomatoes, green beans, and bacon. Bring it to a simmer, cover, and let the chicken cook for 15 to 20 minutes, until the chicken is cooked through. Serve and enjoy.

SWAP: Chicken breasts tend to be used in recipes more frequently than chicken thighs, but I love using thighs. They're cheaper than the white meat and are less likely to dry out.

Per serving: Calories: 388; Total fat: 14g; Total carbs: 16g; Sugar: 6g; Protein: 51g; Fiber: 6g; Sodium: 726mg

Grilled Cilantro-Lime Chicken

People seem to either love or hate cilantro. I'm definitely a fan of the herb, and use it as much as possible in my cooking. I've been making this Grilled Cilantro Lime Chicken for years, and it remains one of my go-to summer dishes. This recipe's simplicity is highlighted by the wonderful herb.

PREP TIME: 10 minutes
COOK TIME: 15 minutes
SERVES: 2

2 tablespoons butter

1 tablespoon minced red onion

2 garlic cloves, minced

Juice of ½ lemon

2 tablespoons chopped fresh cilantro

½ teaspoon Worcestershire sauce

2 boneless skinless chicken breasts

Salt

1. **Prepare.** Preheat the grill to medium-high heat.

2. **Make the cilantro butter.** In a small bowl, mix the butter, onion, garlic, lemon juice, cilantro, and Worcestershire sauce.

3. **Prep and cook the chicken.** Season the chicken breasts with salt and place on the grill. Cook for 5 to 7 minutes on each side, or until the chicken is cooked through.

4. **Top it off.** Top the chicken breasts with a spoonful of cilantro butter, and enjoy.

TIP: The gas grill is one of the most used cooking tools at my house during the warmer months. Not only does it give meat and vegetables a wonderful smoky flavor, but it's also a healthy way to cook, since the fat drips off the food.

SWAP: If you don't like cilantro, you can use parsley or basil instead, in the same quantity as specified.

Per serving: Calories: 350; Total fat: 15g; Total carbs: 2g; Sugar: 1g; Protein: 52g; Fiber: 0g; Sodium: 247mg

One-Skillet Caprese Chicken

During the summer, I like to give every dish I can think of a caprese twist: caprese grilled cheese sandwiches, caprese pasta, caprese orzo salad! Can you tell that I love this flavor combination? This chicken is an easy one-skillet dish that is bursting with that same taste that I can't get enough of.

ONE POT

PREP TIME: 5 minutes
COOK TIME: 25 minutes
SERVES: 2

2 tablespoons extra-virgin olive oil

2 boneless skinless chicken breasts

¼ teaspoon salt

¼ teaspoon freshly ground black pepper

¼ teaspoon garlic powder

¼ cup balsamic vinegar

1 tablespoon honey

1 Roma tomato, sliced

4 ounces fresh mozzarella cheese, sliced

2 tablespoons chopped fresh basil

1. **Cook the chicken.** In an 8- or 9-inch cast-iron skillet over medium-high heat, heat the olive oil. Season the chicken breasts with the salt, pepper, and garlic powder. Add the chicken breasts to the skillet and cook for 6 to 8 minutes on each side, until cooked through.

2. **Make the sauce.** Remove the chicken breasts from the skillet and add the balsamic vinegar and honey, whisking to combine. Cook for 3 minutes, until slightly reduced.

3. **Broil.** Preheat the broiler. Add the chicken back to the skillet, spooning some of the glaze on top of each chicken breast. Top each chicken breast with 2 slices of tomato and 2 slices of mozzarella cheese. Place under the broiler for 1 to 2 minutes, until the cheese is bubbly and golden.

4. **Garnish.** Sprinkle with the fresh chopped basil. Serve and enjoy.

TIP: If you want to speed up this recipe, use a meat tenderizer to pound the chicken into thinner cuts, which will cook faster.

SWAP: Fresh mozzarella packed in water is rich and creamy, and also a little pricey. Feel free to use shredded mozzarella if you need to stay within your food budget.

Per serving: Calories: 541; Total fat: 28g; Total carbs: 14g; Sugar: 11g; Protein: 50g; Fiber: 1g; Sodium: 673mg

Creamy Tuscan Chicken

This chicken is definitely a favorite in my house. The sun-dried tomatoes give the sauce so much depth and flavor, I could seriously eat it with a spoon.

ONE POT

PREP TIME: 10 minutes
COOK TIME: 20 minutes
SERVES: 2

2 boneless skinless chicken breasts

2 tablespoons extra-virgin olive oil

½ white onion, diced

2 garlic cloves, minced

¾ cup heavy cream

½ cup grated Parmesan cheese

¼ cup jarred sun-dried tomatoes in Italian herbs and olive oil, chopped

1 cup fresh baby spinach, chopped

2 tablespoons chopped fresh basil

Salt

Freshly ground black pepper

1. **Prep and cook the chicken.** Pound the chicken into ½-inch-thick slabs. In a medium skillet over medium-high heat, heat the olive oil. Add the chicken and cook for about 5 minutes on each side, until cooked through. Remove the chicken from the skillet.

2. **Make the cream sauce.** Add the onion and garlic to the same skillet, and cook until they're softened, about 5 minutes. Add the heavy cream, Parmesan cheese, sun-dried tomatoes, spinach, and basil. Season with salt and pepper.

3. **Cook.** Cook until the spinach is wilted and the sauce is slightly thickened, about 5 minutes. Return the chicken to the skillet and spoon the sauce over the chicken. Serve and enjoy.

SWAP: Using chopped Tuscan kale instead of spinach will add more texture and flavor to the sauce.

Per serving: Calories: 757; Total fat: 57g; Total carbs: 11g; Sugar: 3g; Protein: 51g; Fiber: 2g; Sodium: 503mg

Greek Roasted Chicken Breasts

Lemons, olives, and oregano are staples in Greek food. The flavors blend together perfectly to create a tasty and aromatic combination. This chicken is best served with a side of roasted potatoes and a salad.

ONE POT

PREP TIME: 10 minutes
COOK TIME: 20 minutes
SERVES: 2

2 boneless skinless chicken breasts

1 cup cherry tomatoes

¼ cup Kalamata olives

1 small red onion, thinly sliced

3 tablespoons extra-virgin olive oil

Juice of 1 lemon

Zest of ½ lemon

½ teaspoon dried oregano

2 garlic cloves, minced

¼ teaspoon salt

¼ teaspoon freshly ground black pepper

¼ cup crumbled feta cheese

1. **Prepare.** Preheat the oven to 425°F. Line a baking sheet with aluminum foil.

2. **Prepare the chicken.** Pound the chicken breasts to ½-inch-thick slabs and place them on the prepared baking sheet, along with the tomatoes, olives, and onion.

3. **Make the marinade.** In a small bowl, combine the olive oil, lemon juice, lemon zest, oregano, garlic, salt, and pepper, and pour the mixture over the chicken breasts and vegetables, stirring well to combine.

4. **Bake the chicken.** Bake in the preheated oven for 20 minutes, until the chicken is cooked through.

5. **Garnish.** Top with the feta cheese. Serve and enjoy.

TIP: Lining your baking pan with aluminum foil helps cut down on cleanup time.

SWAP: Feta cheese is another staple in the Greek diet, but if it's not your favorite, goat cheese will make a fine substitution.

Per serving: Calories: 465; Total fat: 29g; Total carbs: 10g; Sugar: 5g; Protein: 43g; Fiber: 3g; Sodium: 765mg

Garlic Parmesan-Crusted Chicken Tenders

My taste buds may have matured since I was a teenager, but I'll never be too old to enjoy chicken fingers. These Garlic Parmesan-Crusted Chicken tenders are a grown-up version that appeals to my more sophisticated palate. Serve them with a fancy mustard dipping sauce.

PREP TIME: 10 minutes
COOK TIME: 20 minutes
SERVES: 2

Nonstick cooking spray

½ cup shredded
Parmesan cheese

½ cup panko
bread crumbs

½ teaspoon
garlic powder

½ cup all-purpose flour

¼ teaspoon paprika

¼ teaspoon salt

Pinch freshly ground
black pepper

2 eggs

1 pound boneless
skinless chicken tenders

2 tablespoons
butter, melted

1. **Prepare.** Preheat the oven to 400°F. Line a baking sheet with aluminum foil and spray with nonstick cooking spray.

2. **Prepare the chicken coating.** Set out three bowls. In one bowl, combine the Parmesan cheese, bread crumbs, and garlic powder. In the second bowl, mix the flour, paprika, salt, and pepper. In the third bowl, whisk the eggs.

3. **Coat the chicken.** Dip the chicken tenders in the flour, then in the eggs, and then in the bread crumb mixture.

4. **Bake the chicken.** Place the coated chicken tenders onto the prepared baking sheet, and brush them with the butter. Bake in the preheated oven for 15 minutes. Flip the chicken tenders and bake for 5 more minutes.

5. **Serve.** Serve with your favorite dipping sauce.

TIP: If you can't find chicken tenders, buy chicken breasts and cut them into strips.

SWAP: Panko bread crumbs are used in Japanese cooking. They tend to create an extra crispy coating when cooked. However, if you only have regular bread crumbs in your pantry, they will work just as well.

Per serving: Calories: 630; Total fat: 25g; Total carbs: 30g; Sugar: 1g; Protein: 70g; Fiber: 2g; Sodium: 880mg

Coconut Shrimp with Creamy Rémoulade, *page 96*

CHAPTER SIX

SEAFOOD

Seafood is a first-rate healthy option when cooking for two. Fish contains heart-healthy omega-3 fatty acids, and if you opt for an oily fish, such as salmon, you'll also get a good dose of vitamin D. Cooking with fish also resonates with me because of how quickly I can prepare a meal with it. In this chapter you will find everything from Crispy Fish Sandwiches with Herb Tartar Sauce (page 95) to Spicy Salmon Roll Rice Bowls (page 91).

Crab Cakes with Mango Salsa

Fresh shellfish is a treat for us, but it can be hard to procure on a busy weeknight. These delicious crab cakes are made with canned crab meat, which makes them easy and fast. Crab cakes are often served with aioli that I find to be a little too rich. I prefer to make a mango salsa, which brightens up the dish. Plus, any leftover salsa is great with tortilla chips.

PREP TIME: 15 minutes
COOK TIME: 10 minutes
SERVES: 2

⅓ cup bread crumbs

2 tablespoons mayonnaise

1 large egg

2 scallions, chopped, divided

½ teaspoon salt, divided

8 ounces crab meat

1 ripe mango, peeled, pitted, and diced

2 tablespoons chopped fresh cilantro

Juice of ½ lime

1 to 2 tablespoons extra-virgin olive oil

1. **Prepare the crab cake mixture.** In a medium bowl, whisk together the bread crumbs, mayonnaise, egg, half of the chopped scallions, and ¼ teaspoon of salt. Gently fold in the crab meat.

2. **Prepare the salsa.** In a small bowl, mix the diced mango, cilantro, lime juice, the remaining half of the chopped scallions, and the remaining ¼ teaspoon of salt.

3. **Make the crab cakes.** Form the crab mixture into 4 patties, about 1 inch thick and 3 inches in diameter.

4. **Cook the crab cakes.** In a nonstick skillet over medium-high heat, heat the olive oil. Add the patties and cook 4 to 5 minutes on each side, until golden.

5. **Top it off.** Top the crab cakes with mango salsa. Serve and enjoy.

SWAP: Mango can be hard to find, so feel free to use two small peaches in its place. One cup of diced pineapple is also a good substitute.

Per serving: Calories: 445; Total fat: 18g; Total carbs: 45g; Sugar: 4g; Protein: 22g; Fiber: 25g; Sodium: 1662mg

Salmon Cakes with Lemon-Dill-Yogurt Sauce

Canned salmon is an easy source of protein and incredibly versatile. I use it to make salmon salad sandwiches, salmon noodle casserole, and these salmon cakes. The secret to my salmon cakes is to use Ritz crackers, but other crackers will work. Pair these cakes with a side salad or roasted vegetables for a light meal. They also make a great appetizer.

PREP TIME: 15 minutes
COOK TIME: 10 minutes
SERVES: 2

1 (14-ounce) can pink salmon

1 large egg

2 scallions, chopped

½ cup crushed Ritz crackers, or preferred brand

2 tablespoons freshly squeezed lemon juice, divided

½ teaspoon salt, divided

2 tablespoons extra-virgin olive oil

½ cup plain Greek yogurt

Zest of 1 lemon

1 tablespoon fresh dill, minced

1 garlic clove, minced

1. **Prepare the salmon cake mixture.** In a medium bowl, mix the salmon, egg, scallions, crushed crackers, and 1 tablespoon of lemon juice. Season with ¼ teaspoon of salt. Form into 4 equal patties.

2. **Cook the salmon cakes.** In a medium skillet over medium-high heat, heat the olive oil. When the oil is hot, add the salmon patties. Cook for 4 to 5 minutes on each side, until golden and crispy.

3. **Make the lemon dill yogurt sauce.** In a medium bowl, whisk together the yogurt, the remaining 1 table-spoon of lemon juice, lemon zest, dill, garlic, and the remaining ¼ teaspoon of salt.

4. **Top it off.** Top the salmon patties with the yogurt sauce. Serve and enjoy.

SWAP: If you don't want to use Ritz crackers, go ahead and use premade bread crumbs. Crushed potato chips also work well for this recipe.

Per serving: Calories: 539; Total fat: 14g; Total carbs: 23g; Sugar: 8g; Protein: 57g; Fiber: 1g; Sodium: 1067mg

Spicy Salmon Roll Rice Bowls

Before I met my husband, happy hour at my local sushi bar was the go-to for my girl-friends and me. Since my husband isn't a big fan of sushi, I don't get to indulge in it quite as much anymore. But not to worry! On nights when he's working late, I invite a friend over and make us this delicious homemade sushi bowl.

PREP TIME: 15 minutes
COOK TIME: 15 minutes
SERVES: 2

1 tablespoon rice wine vinegar

2 tablespoons soy sauce

1 tablespoon sesame oil

3 tablespoons sriracha, divided

1 pound sushi-grade salmon, cut into bite-size pieces

1 cup white rice

½ cup mayonnaise

1 avocado, peeled, pitted, and sliced

1 small cucumber, peeled and cut into bite-size pieces

1. **Prep the salmon.** In a small bowl, mix the vinegar, soy sauce, sesame oil, and 1 tablespoon of sriracha. Add the salmon pieces and mix thoroughly. Set aside in the refrigerator until you are ready to assemble the bowls.

2. **Cook the rice.** In a small pot over medium-high heat, cook the rice according to package instructions.

3. **Make the spicy mayonnaise.** In a small bowl, mix the mayonnaise and the remaining 2 tablespoons of sriracha.

4. **Assemble.** Divide the rice between two bowls. Top with the avocado, cucumber, salmon, and spicy mayonnaise. Serve and enjoy.

SWAP: Raw fish is an acquired taste. If you've never been a fan, cooked salmon is a perfect substitute.

TIP: If you have leftover spicy mayonnaise, store it in the refrigerator to use on sandwiches for a delicious twist.

Per serving: Calories: 1076; Total fat: 52g; Total carbs: 102g; Sugar: 10g; Protein: 56g; Fiber: 6g; Sodium: 1985mg

Fish Taco Rice Bowls

In graduate school, my study buddies and I used to live off of cheap burrito bowls. They were quick, easy, and relatively healthy compared with other fast food we could've been eating. These days I prefer to make my own, and these fish taco bowls are one of my favorites. We top ours with salsa and cilantro, but feel free to get creative with the toppings—guacamole, sour cream, and cheese are all great options.

PREP TIME: 10 minutes
COOK TIME: 15 minutes
SERVES: 2

½ cup white rice

1 tablespoon butter

Juice of 1 lime, divided

¼ cup chopped fresh cilantro, divided

2 (4-5 ounce) tilapia fillets

½ teaspoon chili powder

½ teaspoon cumin

1 cup canned black beans, drained and rinsed

1 cup salsa

1. **Make the rice.** In a small pot over medium-high heat, cook the rice according to package instructions. Once the rice is cooked, combine with the butter, half of the lime juice, and 2 tablespoons of cilantro.

2. **Prepare the fish.** While the rice is cooking, season the fish fillets with the chili powder, cumin, and the remaining half of the lime juice.

3. **Cook the fish.** In a medium skillet over medium-high heat, heat the olive oil. Add the fish fillets and cook for 2 to 4 minutes on each side, until the fish is no longer transluscent.

4. **Assemble the rice bowls.** Divide the rice between two bowls. Top with the fish, black beans, salsa, and remaining 2 tablespoons of cilantro. Serve and enjoy.

TIP: Make a double batch of rice to have leftovers for Pork Fried Rice (page 111).

SWAP: This recipe calls for tilapia, but any type of white fish can be used. It's really just a matter of preference.

Per serving: Calories: 528; Total fat: 9g; Total carbs: 68g; Sugar: 5g; Protein: 46g; Fiber: 11g; Sodium: 938mg

Shrimp Tacos

Shrimp are the perfect ingredient for a weeknight meal because they cook so quickly. These shrimp tacos are prepped in 5 minutes and cooked in less than 15 minutes. We top ours with sour cream, but avocado, sliced radishes, and cilantro are all delicious options, too.

SUPER QUICK

PREP TIME: 5 minutes
COOK TIME: 15 minutes
SERVES: 2

Nonstick cooking spray

8 ounces shrimp, shelled, deveined, and tails removed

1 small red onion, sliced

1 cup frozen corn

1 teaspoon chili powder

½ teaspoon cumin

½ teaspoon garlic powder

¼ teaspoon salt

2 tablespoons extra-virgin olive oil

4 taco-size tortillas

Sour cream, for topping

1. **Prepare.** Preheat the oven to 450°F. Line a baking sheet with aluminum foil and spray it with nonstick cooking spray.

2. **Prepare the shrimp and vegetables.** In a large bowl, mix together the shrimp, onion, corn, chili powder, cumin, garlic powder, salt, and olive oil. Spread out the shrimp and vegetables on the prepared baking sheet.

3. **Bake.** Bake in the preheated oven for 10 to 15 minutes, until the shrimp is cooked through and the veggies are softened.

4. **Warm the tortillas.** Wrap the tortillas in aluminum foil and place in the oven for the last 4 minutes of baking time.

5. **Assemble.** Place the shrimp and vegetables on the warm tortillas. Top with sour cream and enjoy.

TIP: Frozen shrimp work great in this recipe. Simply run the frozen shrimp under cold water for a few minutes prior to preparing the dish. Just be sure to buy the kind that have been deveined and peeled.

SWAP: Bay scallops make for a great swap here. They're smaller than regular sea scallops and have a similar cook time to the shrimp.

Per serving: Calories: 420; Total fat: 20g; Total carbs: 37g; Sugar: 3g; Protein: 29g; Fiber: 6g; Sodium: 611mg

Cajun Shrimp with Corn Maque Choux

Corn maque choux (pronounced "mock shoe") is the Cajun version of succotash. Traditionally it is made with bacon, but I've removed that from this recipe to keep it simple. The shrimp is cooked in Cajun seasoning, which can be found in the spice aisle at your local grocery store. Season this dish with salt and pepper to your preference, as different Cajun seasoning brands have varying levels of sodium.

PREP TIME: 15 minutes
COOK TIME: 15 minutes
SERVES: 2

2 tablespoons butter, divided

1 small white onion, diced

1 small red bell pepper, stemmed, seeded, and diced

2 cups frozen corn

⅓ cup heavy whipping cream

1 teaspoon dried thyme

1 teaspoon Frank's RedHot sauce

8 ounces shrimp, shelled, deveined, and tails removed

2 teaspoons Cajun seasoning

1. **Cook the vegetables.** In a medium skillet over medium-high heat, melt 1 tablespoon of butter. Add the onion and bell pepper. Cook until the onion is softened, about 5 minutes. Add the corn and cook for another 2 to 3 minutes.

2. **Finish the maque choux.** Add the heavy whipping cream, thyme, and hot sauce to the corn mixture. Reduce the heat to low.

3. **Cook the shrimp.** Heat the remaining 1 tablespoon of butter in another skillet over medium-high heat. Add the shrimp and Cajun seasoning. Cook the shrimp for about 5 minutes.

4. **Assemble.** Top the corn maque choux with the Cajun shrimp. Serve and enjoy.

TIP: While I prefer to not use bacon in my version of this dish, you don't have to abide by my way. Feel free to start with a chopped slice of bacon instead of the butter for an extra boost of flavor.

SWAP: I use frozen corn in the recipe, but if fresh corn is available, I encourage you to use that instead. Simply cut the raw corn off the cob and add it to the onion and bell pepper for an additional 5 minutes of cooking time. Also, you can replace the Frank's sauce with any hot pepper sauce of your choice.

Per serving: Calories: 440; Total fat: 28g; Total carbs: 24g; Sugar: 6g; Protein: g; Fiber: 4g; Sodium: 668mg

Crispy Fish Sandwiches with Herb Tartar Sauce

When my husband and I lived in Seattle, we became obsessed with a hole-in-the-wall fish-and-chips place near our home. Their fish sandwiches are incredible, and I've done my best to recreate them here. The key ingredients are a good potato bun and home-made tartar sauce. This dish takes us back to Seattle every time we have it.

PREP TIME: 15 minutes
COOK TIME: 15 minutes
SERVES: 2

2 (4-ounce) tilapia fillets

2 tablespoons all-purpose flour

1 large egg, lightly beaten

¼ cup cornmeal

2 tablespoons extra-virgin olive oil

½ cup mayonnaise

1 tablespoon sweet pickle relish

1 tablespoon fresh dill, chopped

¼ teaspoon salt

2 potato buns

1. **Prepare.** Preheat the oven to 425°F.

2. **Prep the tilapia.** Set out three bowls. Place the flour in one bowl, the beaten egg in the second bowl, and the cornmeal in the third bowl. Dip each tilapia fillet in the flour, then the egg, then the cornmeal. Place the fillets on a platter.

3. **Cook the fish.** In a medium skillet over medium-high heat, heat the olive oil. Add the fish to the skillet and cook for 2 to 3 minutes on each side, until both sides are golden brown. Place the skillet in the preheated oven for 5 to 7 more minutes, until cooked through.

4. **Make the herb tartar sauce.** While the fish is baking, in a small bowl, combine the mayonnaise, pickle relish, dill, and salt. Whisk to combine.

5. **Serve.** Place the fish on the buns and top with tartar sauce. Serve and enjoy.

SWAP: Brioche buns work well here if you can't find potato buns. Both types of buns are more substantial than regular hamburger buns, yet still light and fluffy.

Per serving: Calories: 602; Total fat: 25g; Total carbs: 65g; Sugar: 10g; Protein: 33g; Fiber: 5g; Sodium: 1103mg

Coconut Shrimp with Creamy Rémoulade

These sweet and savory coconut shrimp are crispy and tender. After one bite, I'm sure you'll want to make this dish again and again. These work well as a meal or an appetizer. For a full meal, pair them with a salad and some bread.

PREP TIME: 15 minutes
COOK TIME: 10 minutes
SERVES: 2

Nonstick cooking spray

¼ cup all-purpose flour

¼ teaspoon salt

¼ teaspoon freshly ground black pepper

1 large egg, beaten

½ cup panko bread crumbs

½ cup sweetened shredded coconut

8 ounces shrimp, shelled, deveined, and tails removed

¼ cup mayonnaise

2 tablespoons Thai chili sauce

½ teaspoon onion powder

1. **Prepare.** Preheat the oven to 400°F. Line a baking sheet with aluminum foil and spray it with nonstick cooking spray.

2. **Prepare the shrimp coating.** Set out three bowls. In one bowl, mix the flour, salt, and pepper. In the second bowl, whisk the egg. In the third bowl, combine the bread crumbs and coconut.

3. **Coat the shrimp.** Dip each shrimp in the flour, then dredge in the egg, then coat with the bread crumb mixture.

4. **Bake.** Place the shrimp on the prepared baking sheet and bake for 10 minutes.

5. **Make the rémoulade.** In a small bowl, combine the mayonnaise, Thai chili sauce, and onion powder, stirring to combine.

6. **Serve.** Serve the shrimp with the rémoulade.

SWAP: If you want to cut back on the sugar content, use unsweetened shredded coconut.

Per serving: Calories: 479; Total fat: 22g; Total carbs: 39g; Sugar: 17g; Protein: 30g; Fiber: 2g; Sodium: 1458mg

Chili-Lime Shrimp Skewers

These skewers are perfect for a summer backyard barbecue. I add lime zest to the lime juice marinade for an extra citrusy punch. On the grill, the marinade will caramelize, giving the shrimp a rich, smoky-sweet flavor.

SUPER QUICK

PREP TIME: 10 minutes
COOK TIME: 6 minutes
SERVES: 2

4 tablespoons freshly squeezed lime juice, divided

2 teaspoons grated lime zest

2 tablespoons extra-virgin olive oil

½ teaspoon chili powder

½ teaspoon cumin

2 garlic cloves, minced

2 tablespoons chopped fresh cilantro

¼ teaspoon salt

1 pound raw shrimp, shelled, deveined, and tails removed

1. **Prepare.** Preheat the grill to medium-high heat.

2. **Mix the marinade.** In a small bowl, stir together 3 tablespoons of lime juice, the lime zest, olive oil, chili powder, cumin, garlic, cilantro, and salt.

3. **Prepare the shrimp.** Thread the shrimp onto metal skewers and coat with the marinade.

4. **Cook the shrimp.** Place the shrimp on the grill and cook until slightly charred and cooked through, 2 to 3 minutes on each side.

5. **Drizzle.** Drizzle the remaining 1 tablespoon of lime juice over the shrimp. Serve and enjoy.

SWAP: I really like the way lime works with shrimp in this dish. But if you have only lemons on hand, use them. The shrimp will be slightly less tangy, but still delicious.

Per serving: Calories: 253; Total fat: 15g; Total carbs: 6g; Sugar: 1g; Protein: 24g; Fiber: 1g; Sodium: 554mg

Mediterranean Salmon Kabobs

Traditional shish kabobs are usually very meat heavy. This recipe offers a delicious take on the old standby—even my meat-and-potatoes–loving husband raves about it. When shopping for your salmon for this recipe, try to find thick slices, since bigger chunks will be easier to thread on skewers.

PREP TIME: 15 minutes
COOK TIME: 10 minutes
SERVES: 2

2 (6-ounce) salmon fillets, skin removed and cut into 1-inch pieces

5 tablespoons extra-virgin olive oil, divided

2 teaspoons dried oregano

2 garlic cloves, minced

½ teaspoon salt, divided

Pinch freshly ground black pepper

Juice and zest of 1 lemon

1 small zucchini, cut into 1-inch pieces

1 red bell pepper, seeded and cut into 1-inch chunks

1 yellow or orange bell pepper, seeded and cut into 1-inch chunks

1. **Prepare.** Preheat the grill to medium-high heat.

2. **Prepare the salmon.** In a medium bowl, combine the salmon, 3 tablespoons of olive oil, the oregano, garlic, ¼ teaspoon of salt, pepper, lemon juice, and lemon zest.

3. **Prepare the vegetables.** In another medium bowl, toss the zucchini and bell peppers in the remaining 2 tablespoons of olive oil and season with the remaining ¼ teaspoon of salt.

4. **Assemble the kabobs.** Thread 2 to 4 skewers, depending on how long they are, alternating the salmon, zucchini, and bell peppers.

5. **Grill the kabobs.** Place the skewers on the grill and cook for 4 to 5 minutes. Turn and cook another 3 to 4 minutes. Serve and enjoy.

SWAP: Any type of firm fish, such as cod or swordfish, will work well here just as well. You want the fish to be able to retain its shape and not fall off the skewers once it's been cooked.

Per serving: Calories: 726; Total fat: 45g; Total carbs: 12g; Sugar: 6g; Protein: 70g; Fiber: 3g; Sodium: 773mg

One-Pan Honey-Ginger Salmon and Vegetables

One-pan dinners are convenient, but they also require coordination because everything needs to cook at the same time. For this salmon and vegetable dinner, I use softer vegetables, like zucchini and thinly sliced bell pepper, so that each element cooks at the same rate. This is a satisfying meal by itself, but if you want to round it out, serve it with a side of quinoa or rice.

ONE POT

PREP TIME: 10 minutes
COOK TIME: 20 minutes
SERVES: 2

Nonstick cooking spray

2 (6-ounce) salmon fillets

1 large zucchini, halved lengthwise and cut into ¼-inch semicircles

1 red bell pepper, seeded and cut into thin strips

¼ cup honey

3 tablespoons soy sauce

2 tablespoons extra-virgin olive oil

1 teaspoon minced fresh ginger

1 garlic clove, minced

1. **Prepare.** Preheat the oven to 400°F. Line a baking sheet with aluminum foil and spray it with nonstick cooking spray.

2. **Prepare the salmon and vegetables.** Place the salmon, zucchini, and bell pepper onto the prepared baking sheet.

3. **Make the honey ginger sauce.** In a small bowl, whisk together the honey, soy sauce, olive oil, ginger, and garlic. Pour three fourths of the sauce over the salmon and vegetables, and stir so it is evenly distributed.

4. **Bake the salmon and vegetables.** Bake in the preheated oven for 15 to 18 minutes, until the salmon easily flakes.

5. **Serve.** Pour the remaining sauce over the salmon and vegetables, and enjoy.

TIP: Try to buy salmon fillets that are the same thickness all the way across to ensure even cooking.

SWAP: If you want to use other vegetables, broccoli and carrots chopped into very small pieces are good options.

Per serving: Calories: 612; Total fat: 32g; Total carbs: 48g; Sugar: 41g; Protein: 37g; Fiber: 3g; Sodium: 1470mg

Skillet Lemon Scallop Piccata

Chicken piccata is a traditional dish in many places, but I prefer this scallop piccata because it's a little more unique. The flavor and texture the fish brings are unbeatable. The dish is light yet indulgent, and is ideal on top of angel hair pasta. This is a delicious meal for date night in.

PREP TIME: 10 minutes
COOK TIME: 15 minutes
SERVES: 2

4 ounces angel hair pasta

12 ounces large scallops

¼ teaspoon salt

¼ teaspoon freshly ground black pepper

2 tablespoons butter, divided

1 tablespoon extra-virgin olive oil

2 garlic cloves, minced

½ cup white wine

1 tablespoon capers

2 tablespoons freshly squeezed lemon juice

1 teaspoon grated lemon zest

1 tablespoon chopped fresh parsley, plus more for serving

1. **Cook the pasta.** Bring a medium pot of water to a boil. Add the pasta and cook according to package instructions. Drain and set aside.

2. **Prep the scallops.** While the pasta is cooking, pat the scallops dry with a paper towel and season with the salt and pepper.

3. **Cook the scallops.** In a large skillet over high heat, melt 1 tablespoon of butter and add the olive oil. Once the oil and butter are hot, add the scallops to the skillet and cook until browned, 2 to 3 minutes on each side. Remove the scallops from the skillet and cover loosely on a plate.

4. **Make the sauce.** Add the garlic to the skillet and combine with the juice from the scallops. Cook for 1 minute over medium-high heat. Add the wine, capers, lemon juice, and lemon zest, using a spatula to scrape up the garlic and drippings. Cook for another 3 to 4 minutes, until slightly reduced. Add the remaining 1 tablespoon of butter and the parsley, and stir until the butter is melted.

5. **Assemble the scallops.** Return the scallops to the pan, and spoon the sauce over them. Divide the cooked pasta between two plates. Place the scallops on top of the cooked pasta. Drizzle any extra sauce from the pan, and top with parsley. Serve and enjoy.

TIP: The key to perfect scallops is to pat them dry prior to cooking. Also make sure to cook them only for a couple of minutes on each side. If you cook them for too long, they become rubbery.

SWAP: The wine in this recipe brings a nice depth to the sauce, but it isn't necessary. You can use vegetable broth instead to deglaze the pan.

Per serving: Calories: 582; Total fat: 21g; Total carbs: 49g; Sugar: 3g; Protein: 36g; Fiber: 2g; Sodium: 868mg

Baked Cod with Gremolata

Gremolata is a classic Italian condiment that's full of flavor. It's traditionally made with parsley, garlic, and lemon zest. I add bread crumbs to mine to give the baked fish a beautiful golden-green topping.

PREP TIME: 10 minutes
COOK TIME: 15 minutes
SERVES: 2

2 (4-ounce) cod fillets

2 teaspoons extra-virgin olive oil, divided

½ teaspoon salt, divided

½ teaspoon freshly ground black pepper

¼ cup chopped fresh parsley

2 tablespoons bread crumbs

2 garlic cloves, minced

Zest of 1 lemon

1. **Prepare.** Preheat the oven to 400°F. Line a baking sheet with parchment paper.

2. **Prepare the cod.** Place the cod fillets on the prepared baking sheet. Brush the cod fillets with 1 teaspoon of olive oil, and sprinkle with ¼ teaspoon of salt and the pepper.

3. **Make the gremolata.** In a small bowl, mix the parsley, the remaining 1 teaspoon of olive oil, garlic, lemon zest, and remaining ¼ teaspoon of salt. Divide evenly between the two cod fillets.

4. **Bake the cod.** Bake in the preheated oven for 15 minutes, until it's white and easily flaked. Serve and enjoy.

TIP: If you're using frozen cod, be sure to thaw it in the refrigerator a day in advance. If the cod is still frozen on the inside, it will add an extra 10 to 15 minutes to the baking time.

SWAP: If garlic is too pungent for you, use 1 small shallot instead. You can also swap the parsley for any other herbs that you have on hand.

Per serving: Calories: 165; Total fat: 6g; Total carbs: 7g; Sugar: 1g; Protein: 21g; Fiber: 1g; Sodium: 706mg

Lemon-Butter Salmon and Orzo

When people tell me they don't like salmon, I can't help but think they just haven't had it prepared correctly. There's a fine line between perfectly cooked and overcooked salmon. I've found that cooking it at a higher temperature for a shorter amount of time is the key to achieving tender salmon. Basting it with lemon butter adds flavor and a bit of fat, which also keeps the salmon from getting dried out. The lemon butter is used twice—for basting and as a sauce in the orzo—which makes the prep for this dish super easy.

PREP TIME: 5 minutes
COOK TIME: 20 minutes
SERVES: 2

3 tablespoons butter

Juice of ½ lemon

1 teaspoon grated lemon zest

2 garlic cloves, minced

¼ teaspoon salt

2 (6-ounce) salmon fillets

¾ cup orzo

½ cup shredded Parmesan cheese

2 tablespoons chopped fresh parsley

1. **Prepare.** Preheat the oven to 425°F. Line a baking sheet with aluminum foil.

2. **Make the lemon butter.** In a microwave-safe bowl, microwave the butter on high for 30 seconds. Add the lemon juice, lemon zest, garlic, and salt. Stir to combine.

3. **Bake the salmon.** Place the salmon fillets on the prepared baking sheet. Drizzle 1 tablespoon of the lemon butter over each fillet. Bake in the preheated oven for 12 to 15 minutes, until the salmon flakes easily.

4. **Cook the orzo.** While the salmon is cooking, bring a small pot of water to a boil. Add the orzo and cook according to package instructions, about 10 minutes. Once the orzo is cooked, drain the water and put the pasta back in the pot.

5. **Finish the orzo.** Add the remaining lemon butter and the Parmesan cheese to the orzo and stir well to combine.

6. **Top it off.** Top the orzo with the salmon and fresh parsley. Serve and enjoy.

SWAP: Any small shaped pasta, such as ditalini or orecchiette, will work well for this dish.

Per serving: Calories: 593; Total fat: 42g; Total carbs: 20g; Sugar: 1g; Protein: 34g; Fiber: 2g; Sodium: 737mg

Pistachio-Crusted Halibut

If you're looking for an impressive dish that isn't difficult to prepare, look no further. This pistachio-crusted halibut is easy enough for a beginner to cook, but fancy and tasty enough for a Christmas dinner. This dish also pairs well with potatoes and roasted vegetables.

SUPER QUICK

PREP TIME: 5 minutes
COOK TIME: 15 minutes
SERVES: 2

Nonstick cooking spray

¼ cup shelled unsalted pistachios

2 tablespoons bread crumbs

1 garlic clove, minced

1 tablespoon butter, melted

¼ teaspoon salt

2 (6-ounce) halibut fillets

1 tablespoon Dijon mustard

1. **Prepare.** Preheat the oven to 400°F. Spray a small baking dish with nonstick cooking spray.

2. **Prepare the pistachio topping.** In a food processor, combine the pistachios, bread crumbs, garlic, melted butter, and salt. Pulse until it resembles coarse crumbs.

3. **Prepare the halibut.** Place the halibut fillets in the baking dish and spread the mustard over the fillets. Press the pistachio mixture on top.

4. **Bake.** Bake the halibut in the preheated oven for 10 to 12 minutes, until the halibut flakes easily. Serve and enjoy.

TIP: If you use salted pistachios, adjust the amount of salt listed in the ingredients accordingly.

SWAP: I like to use halibut to make this dish, but I've also tried tilapia and cod with equally delicious results.

Per serving: Calories: 280; Total fat: 12g; Total carbs: 7g; Sugar: 1g; Protein: 36g; Fiber: 1g; Sodium: 561mg

Grilled Sesame-Crusted Tuna Steaks

I used to eat seared tuna only at restaurants until I realized how easy it is to prepare at home. This grilled tuna is marinated in a simple mixture of soy sauce, sesame oil, rice wine vinegar, and fresh ginger, and then coated in sesame seeds. Just a few minutes on the grill is all the steaks need to be perfectly seared on the outside and rare on the inside.

SUPER QUICK

PREP TIME: 10 minutes
COOK TIME: 6 minutes
SERVES: 2

2 tablespoons soy sauce

1 tablespoon sesame oil

1 tablespoon rice
wine vinegar

1 teaspoon minced
fresh ginger

2 (6-ounce) tuna steaks

¼ cup sesame seeds

2 tablespoons chopped
scallions

1. **Prepare the marinade.** In a medium bowl, whisk together the soy sauce, sesame oil, vinegar, and ginger. Place the tuna steaks in a small plastic container and pour the mixture over them. Let it sit for 10 minutes.

2. **Preheat the grill to medium-high heat.**

3. **Prepare the tuna steaks.** Remove the tuna from the container and place it on a flat surface. Press the sesame seeds onto the tuna steaks.

4. **Grill the tuna.** Place the tuna steaks on the grill and cook for 2 to 3 minutes on each side, depending on your preference of doneness, watching the steaks closely.

5. **Garnish.** Top the tuna with the scallions. Serve and enjoy.

TIP: This recipe creates tuna with a rare center. For a medium-rare center, cook for 1 to 2 more minutes on each side.

SWAP: Soy sauce contains wheat, so if you're abiding by a gluten-free diet, opt for tamari instead. It's pure soy sauce—with no wheat additives.

Per serving: Calories: 351; Total fat: 16g; Total carbs: 7g; Sugar: 1g; Protein: 46g; Fiber: 3g; Sodium: 1056mg

Chimichurri Grilled Steak, *page 123*

CHAPTER SEVEN

MEAT

When it comes to cooking, I like to experiment with new ingredients and different cooking styles. But I'm also a big fan of the classics. In this chapter I've done my best to pair tradition and innovation. Here you'll find plenty of recipes that offer a fresh take on classic dishes, such as beef stroganoff, teriyaki stir-fry, stuffed cabbage rolls, steak fajitas, and many more.

Crunchy Beef Tostadas

I love tacos just as much as the next girl, but sometimes I need to switch it up. These crunchy beef tostadas are similar to an open-faced sandwich and can be eaten with a knife and fork. Or just go ahead and use your hands . . . no one is watching! You might love these so much that Taco Tuesday will turn into Tostada Tuesday.

PREP TIME: 10 minutes
COOK TIME: 20 minutes
SERVES: 2

8 ounces lean ground beef, 10 percent fat

1 tablespoon taco seasoning

¼ cup water

4 corn tostada shells

½ cup refried beans

½ cup shredded Mexican cheese blend

½ cup shredded iceberg lettuce

½ cup pico de gallo

1. **Cook the beef.** In a medium skillet over medium-high, cook the ground beef until it is thoroughly browned and no longer pink.

2. **Season the beef.** Add the taco seasoning and water. Cook for another 2 to 3 minutes, until the sauce starts to thicken.

3. **Assemble the tostadas.** Top each tostada shell with 2 tablespoons of refried beans. Then top with the taco meat, cheese, lettuce, and pico de gallo. Serve and enjoy.

SWAP: Pico de gallo is great because of how fresh it tastes, but a jar of salsa will also work well.

Per serving: Calories: 403; Total fat: 12g; Total carbs: 41g; Sugar: 4g; Protein: 30g; Fiber: 7g; Sodium: 1103mg

Hawaiian Steak Kabobs

Did you know that meat kabobs originated with medieval soldiers who used their swords to cook meat over an open fire? These days we use skewers instead of swords, but the method of cutting meat into small chunks still remains a great way to cut back on cooking time. In this recipe, the kabobs get a quick marinade in teriyaki sauce and then cook up quickly on the grill, making them a great summer meal.

5-INGREDIENT

PREP TIME: 15 minutes
COOK TIME: 12 minutes
SERVES: 2

1 (12-ounce) sirloin steak

¼ cup teriyaki sauce, plus extra for finishing

1 cup cubed pineapple (1-inch cubes)

½ green bell pepper, seeded and cut into 1-inch squares

1 small red or white onion, cut into 1-inch cubes

1. **Prepare.** Preheat the grill to medium-high heat.

2. **Prep the steak.** Cut the steak into 1-inch cubes and place in a bowl. Toss the steak with the teriyaki sauce.

3. **Assemble the kabobs.** Thread the beef, pineapple, bell pepper, and onion onto 4 metal skewers.

4. **Grill the kabobs.** Place the skewers on the grill and cook for 2 to 3 minutes on each side.

5. **Top it off.** Brush with extra teriyaki sauce. Serve and enjoy.

TIP: Use metal skewers so you don't have to waste time soaking wooden skewers prior to cooking.

SWAP: Swap the sirloin for your favorite cut of beef. Add any of your favorite vegetables to these kabobs; zucchini, mushrooms, and green bell peppers are all great.

Per serving: Calories: 309; Total fat: 7g; Total carbs: 19g; Sugar: 15g; Protein: 41g; Fiber: 2g; Sodium: 1382mg

Pork Fried Rice

Fried rice has been a staple in my kitchen for years, but I just recently began adding ground pork to it. Ground pork is an excellent but underused protein, often overshadowed by ground beef or chicken, that easily soaks up the flavors of garlic, ginger, and soy sauce. Since this fried rice includes a starch, vegetables, and a protein, it's a complete meal in itself!

SUPER QUICK

PREP TIME: 5 minutes
COOK TIME: 15 minutes
SERVES: 2

½ tablespoon sesame oil

8 ounces ground pork

2 cups cooked rice

1½ cups frozen mixed vegetables with peas, corn, and carrots

1 teaspoon minced fresh ginger

2 garlic cloves, minced

2 tablespoons soy sauce

1 large egg

2 scallions, chopped

1. **Cook the pork.** In a large skillet over medium-high heat, heat the sesame oil. Add the ground pork and cook, breaking it up with a wooden spatula as it cooks, 5 to 7 minutes. You don't need to salt it at this point, as the soy sauce will lend to its overall saltiness.

2. **Add the rice and vegetables.** In the skillet, add the cooked rice, mixed vegetables, ginger, garlic, and soy sauce. Cook over medium-high heat for 5 minutes, until the vegetables are warmed through. If you want your rice a little extra crispy, cook for an additional 4 to 5 minutes.

3. **Add the egg.** Make a well in the middle of the rice mixture and add the egg. Beat the egg with your spatula to scramble. Let it cook in the middle of the mixture, stirring a few times to keep scrambling the egg. Once the egg is cooked, combine it with the rice mixture.

4. **Garnish.** Top with the scallions. Serve and enjoy.

TIP: Leftover rice is actually better than fresh rice when making this dish. Because the rice is drier, it will soak up more flavor; plus, it saves time because you don't have to wait for the rice to cook.

SWAP: Ground chicken, ground turkey, or even thinly sliced pork chops make excellent protein substitutions for this dish.

Per serving: Calories: 589; Total fat: 17g; Total carbs: 70g; Sugar: 7g; Protein: 34g; Fiber: 5g; Sodium: 1039mg

Thai Peanut Beef

I really love the flavors of Thai food—everything from curries to peanut sauce. This Thai peanut beef is no exception. It's hard to believe a dish that is so easy and fast to prepare has so much flavor. I prefer to serve this with white or brown rice.

SUPER QUICK

PREP TIME: 5 minutes
COOK TIME: 10 minutes
SERVES: 2

1 tablespoon vegetable or canola oil

1 pound flank steak, thinly sliced, or stir-fry beef

¼ cup peanut butter

2 tablespoons soy sauce

1 tablespoon honey

2 to 3 teaspoons sriracha, depending on your spice tolerance

¼ cup chopped peanuts

2 tablespoons scallions

1. **Cook the steak.** In a medium skillet over medium-high heat, heat the oil. Add the steak slices and cook until browned, about 4 minutes per side.

2. **Make the peanut sauce.** In a small bowl, whisk together the peanut butter, soy sauce, honey, and sriracha.

3. **Combine.** Add the peanut butter mixture to the cooked beef and stir well to combine.

4. **Serve.** Top with the peanuts and scallions and enjoy. Serve over white or brown rice, if desired, for an even more filling meal.

TIP: Adding steamed broccoli to this dish rounds it out as a complete meal.

SWAP: For an additional boost of protein, serve this over quinoa. The grain (which is technically a seed) has 8 grams of protein per serving.

Per serving: Calories: 794; Total fat: 52g; Total carbs: 21g; Sugar: 13g; Protein: 63g; Fiber: 4g; Sodium: 1090mg

Teriyaki Beef Stir-Fry

In my household, takeout is one of our biggest guilty pleasures. We love beef stir-fry in particular, but to save our wallets and our sodium levels, we try to limit how often we order it in. To compensate, I've come up with a dish that recreates what we order, and it hits the spot every time.

PREP TIME: 10 minutes
COOK TIME: 15 minutes
SERVES: 2

3 tablespoons soy sauce

¼ cup plus
2 tablespoons
water, divided

2 tablespoons
brown sugar

2 garlic cloves, minced

2 teaspoons minced
fresh ginger

1 teaspoon sesame oil

1 tablespoon cornstarch

1 tablespoon extra-virgin
olive oil

1 (12-ounce) flank steak,
thinly sliced

2 cups fresh precut,
mixed stir-fry vegetables

Rice or noodles,
for serving

1. **Make the teriyaki sauce.** In a small saucepan over medium-high heat, combine the soy sauce, ¼ cup of water, brown sugar, garlic, ginger, and sesame oil. Bring to a boil, reduce the heat, and simmer for 3 minutes. In a small bowl, whisk together the cornstarch and the remaining 2 tablespoons of water. Stir into the saucepan and cook for 2 more minutes. Remove from the heat.

2. **Cook the beef and vegetables.** In a large skillet over medium-high heat, heat the olive oil. Add the steak and mixed vegetables, and cook until the beef is cooked through and the vegetables are softened, 7 to 10 minutes.

3. **Combine.** Add the teriyaki sauce to the beef and vegetables. Stir to combine.

4. **Serve.** Serve the stir-fry on top of rice or noodles, and enjoy.

TIP: You can buy your stir-fry vegetables separately, but I like to save time by using precut vegetables for this dish. Most grocery stores carry the combination of broccoli, snow peas, and carrots. Frozen veggies can also work.

SWAP: If you're short on time, use jarred teriyaki sauce. Just add about a ½ cup to the beef and vegetable mixture.

Per serving: Calories: 535; Total fat: 25g; Total carbs: 34g; Sugar: 9g; Protein: 42g; Fiber: 10g; Sodium: 1906mg

Avocado Club Burgers

I love burgers! In my house we love to get creative with our toppings. Avocado and bacon add a richness to these burgers, making them truly decadent. In the summer we like to pair these with corn on the cob, oven-roasted fries, and some fresh watermelon for a well-rounded array of flavors.

PREP TIME: 10 minutes
COOK TIME: 20 minutes
SERVES: 2

4 slices bacon

12 ounces lean ground beef, 10 percent fat

½ teaspoon garlic powder

½ teaspoon Worcestershire sauce

Pinch salt

½ avocado, peeled, pitted, and sliced

1 tomato, sliced

2 romaine or iceberg lettuce leaves

2 hamburger buns

1. **Cook the bacon.** In a medium skillet over medium-high heat, cook the bacon for 5 to 7 minutes, or until it reaches your desired crispiness.

2. **Preheat the grill.** While the bacon is cooking, preheat the grill to medium-high heat.

3. **Prepare the hamburger patties.** In a small bowl, mix the ground beef, garlic powder, and Worcestershire sauce. Season with the salt. Form into 2 patties.

4. **Cook the burgers.** Place the burger patties on the preheated grill and cook for 4 to 5 minutes on each side, or until your preferred doneness.

5. **Assemble.** Place a patty on each bun. Top each burger with avocado, tomato, lettuce, and bacon. Serve and enjoy.

TIP: The garlic fries from Roasted Balsamic Portobello Mushroom Burgers with Garlic Fries (page 64) are also a perfect side for this burger.

SWAP: You can use portobello mushrooms in place of the beef burgers. Simply brush the mushroom caps with Worcestershire sauce, then season with garlic powder and salt. Grill for 3 to 4 minutes on each side.

Per serving: Calories: 664; Total fat: 37g; Total carbs: 28g; Sugar: 4g; Protein: 54g; Fiber: 4g; Sodium: 1286mg

One-Pan Steak Fajitas

Instead of coming out in a hot cast-iron skillet, these fajitas come out on a baking sheet. Everything, from the veggies to the steak, is tossed in the same spice mixture and cooked in one pan, making prep and cleanup super easy.

ONE POT

PREP TIME: 10 minutes
COOK TIME: 20 minutes
SERVES: 2

1 (8- to 12-ounce) skirt steak, cut into ¼-inch-thick strips

½ red bell pepper, seeded and thinly sliced

½ green bell pepper, seeded and thinly sliced

½ small red onion, sliced

2 tablespoons extra-virgin olive oil

¼ teaspoon salt

2 teaspoons chili powder

½ teaspoon cumin

½ teaspoon paprika

4 to 6 fajita-size flour tortillas

1. **Prepare.** Preheat the oven to 400°F. Line a large baking sheet with aluminum foil.

2. **Prepare the steak and vegetables.** Place the steak, bell peppers, and onion on the baking sheet. Drizzle the olive oil and sprinkle the salt over the top.

3. **Prepare the spice mix.** In a small bowl, combine the chili powder, cumin, and paprika. Mix well and then sprinkle over the steak and vegetables. Stir to evenly coat.

4. **Cook the fajitas.** Bake in the preheated oven for 20 minutes, until the steak is done and the vegetables are cooked through.

5. **Assemble.** Spoon into the tortillas. Serve and enjoy.

TIP: I like to wrap my tortillas in aluminum foil and place them in the oven for the last 5 minutes of the baking time. Otherwise you can place them on a microwave-safe plate, cover with a damp paper towel, and microwave for 30 to 60 seconds.

SWAP: To spice things up, use a poblano pepper (mildly spicy) or jalapeño pepper (moderately spicy) instead of a green bell pepper.

Per serving: Calories: 452; Total fat: 25g; Total carbs: 29g; Sugar: 4g; Protein: 28g; Fiber: 5g; Sodium: 417mg

One-Pot Cheesy Taco Pasta

This dish has all the flavor of beef tacos, but it's loaded into pasta instead of taco shells. On top of that, it's all made in one pot—my favorite kind of dinner. This is a dish where you can get super creative with your toppings and have a lot of fun.

PREP TIME: 5 minutes
COOK TIME: 25 minutes
SERVES: 2 or 3

8 ounces lean ground beef, 10 percent fat

½ white onion, chopped

3 tablespoons taco seasoning

1 (10-ounce) can diced tomatoes with lime and cilantro

3 to 4 ounces rotini pasta (about 1½ cups)

1¼ cups water

¼ cup sour cream

¾ cup shredded Mexican cheese blend

2 tablespoons diced scallion

1. **Cook the beef and onions.** In a medium pot over medium-high heat, place the ground beef and onion. Cook until the ground beef is brown and the onion is softened, 7 to 8 minutes. Once the beef is cooked, drain the fat.

2. **Cook the pasta.** In a medium saucepan over medium-high heat, combine the taco seasoning, diced tomatoes, pasta, and water. Bring the ingredients to a boil, lower the heat to medium-low, cover, and cook for 10 to 13 minutes, until the pasta is tender. The pasta will soak up the liquid so no draining is required.

3. **Finish the sauce.** Stir in the sour cream and shredded cheese.

4. **Garnish.** Top with the diced scallion. Serve and enjoy.

TIP: The recipe calls for you to top this dish with scallion, but don't be afraid to experiment with avocado, cilantro, or even some hot sauce. Another recipe that uses half of a white onion is Chipotle Lentil Soup (page 43).

SWAP: To add a little extra kick, use canned diced tomatoes that have green chiles.

Per serving: Calories: 601; Total fat: 19g; Total carbs: 70g; Sugar: 12g; Protein: 35g; Fiber: 5g; Sodium: 2048mg

Cheesy Sausage and Ravioli Skillet

I'm responsible for almost all of the cooking in our house. I don't mind because it's a passion of mine, but when my husband does cook, this dish is one of his specialties. Between the meat, sauce, and cheese, this meal is rich in flavor, hearty, and delicious!

ONE POT

PREP TIME: 10 minutes
COOK TIME: 20 minutes
SERVES: 2

8 ounces Italian sausage

1 (24-ounce) jar
marinara sauce

1 teaspoon Italian
seasoning

½ teaspoon
garlic powder

8 to 9 ounces refrigerated
cheese ravioli

¼ cup water

¾ cup shredded Italian
cheese blend

2 tablespoons chopped
fresh basil

1. **Prepare.** Preheat the oven to broil.

2. **Cook the sausage.** In a medium ovenproof skillet over medium-high heat, cook the Italian sausage. Break it up into pieces with a wooden spatula, cooking it all the way through, about 5 minutes.

3. **Cook the ravioli.** Add the marinara sauce, Italian seasoning, garlic powder, ravioli, and water. Bring the mixture to a boil, then reduce the heat to medium-low, and cover. Let it simmer until the ravioli is cooked, about 10 minutes.

4. **Add the cheese.** Sprinkle with the Italian cheese blend, place in the preheated oven, and broil until golden brown, about 2 minutes.

5. **Garnish.** Top with the basil. Serve and enjoy.

TIP: If you have to buy a 1-pound package of Italian sausage, use the ½ pound left over from this recipe to make Skillet Lasagna (page 118).

SWAP: When it comes to stuffed pastas, there aren't many options. Even so, tortellini is an excellent substitute here. It may even hold up a bit better because of its shape, since ravioli has a tendency to stick together more easily than tortellini.

Per serving: Calories: 732; Total fat: 44g; Total carbs: 54g; Sugar: 20g; Protein: 28g; Fiber: 5g; Sodium: 2412mg

Skillet Lasagna

Lasagna is one of those comfort foods that is delicious but can be a lot of work to make. From preboiling the noodles to setting all of the layers, a lot of time goes into making this classic Italian dish. For this version, I took all of the flavors of lasagna and put them into an easy one-dish meal. My favorite part is the dollops of ricotta cheese on top.

ONE POT

PREP TIME: 10 minutes
COOK TIME: 20 minutes
SERVES: 2

1 tablespoon extra-virgin olive oil

8 ounces Italian sausage

½ onion, diced

1 (24-ounce) jar marinara sauce

1 (28-ounce) can crushed tomatoes

½ teaspoon Italian seasoning

¼ teaspoon salt

4 ounces lasagna noodles (about 4 sheets), broken up into small pieces

½ cup ricotta cheese

½ cup shredded mozzarella cheese

1. **Cook the sausage and onion.** In a medium cast-iron skillet over medium-high heat, heat the olive oil. Add the Italian sausage and onion, cooking until the sausage is browned and onion is softened, 5 to 7 minutes.

2. **Cook the noodles.** Once the sausage and onion are cooked, add the marinara sauce, crushed tomatoes, Italian seasoning, salt, and lasagna noodles. Stir well until the lasagna noodles are incorporated into the tomato sauce mixture. Be sure to push the noodles toward the bottom of the pan so they are covered with sauce. Bring to a simmer, cover, and cook until the lasagna noodles are al dente, about 10 minutes. Check often and stir so the noodles do not clump.

3. **Preheat the broiler.** While the noodles are cooking, preheat the broiler.

4. **Broil the lasagna.** Dollop the ricotta cheese into the pan and top with the mozzarella cheese. Place in the broiler and broil until the mozzarella cheese is golden, 1 to 2 minutes. Serve and enjoy.

SWAP: For fewer calories, opt for ground turkey. If you don't want to use Italian sausage in this recipe, ground beef also works well.

Per serving: Calories: 872; Total fat: 44g; Total carbs: 81g; Sugar: 33g; Protein: 39g; Fiber: 18g; Sodium: 2013mg

One-Pot Beef Stroganoff

When I think of nostalgic meals from my childhood, beef stroganoff is without a doubt in my top five. My dad liked to make the beef mixture and serve it on top of mashed potatoes. I prefer mine with noodles. It also gets major bonus points for being made in one pot—you can't beat that.

ONE POT

PREP TIME: 5 minutes
COOK TIME: 20 minutes
SERVES: 2 or 3

1 tablespoon butter

½ white onion, diced

1 garlic clove, minced

8 ounces lean ground beef, 10 percent fat

1 cup sliced mushrooms

1 tablespoon flour

1 tablespoon Worcestershire sauce

2 cups beef broth

4 ounces egg noodles (about 2 cups)

¼ cup sour cream

1. **Cook the onion and garlic.** In a medium pot over medium-high heat, melt the butter. Add the onion and garlic and cook until slightly softened, about 4 minutes.

2. **Cook the beef.** Add the beef to the onion and garlic, and continue cooking until the beef is browned and cooked through, 5 to 7 minutes. Be sure to break up the meat with a spatula as you go.

3. **Cook the mushrooms.** Add the mushrooms and stir. Cook until soft, about 5 minutes.

4. **Add the flour.** Add the flour and stir to combine. Cook for another minute.

5. **Add the beef broth.** Stir in the Worcestershire sauce and beef broth with a whisk to combine with the flour.

6. **Cook the noodles.** Add the noodles and bring to a simmer. Cover and let the mixture simmer for 10 minutes, or until the noodles are softened.

7. **Add the sour cream.** Stir in the sour cream. Serve and enjoy.

TIP: I've seen beef stroganoff made with ground beef and cubed round beef, and this recipe can be made with either.

SWAP: To cut back on the fat content, use fat-free Greek yogurt instead of sour cream.

Per serving: Calories: 509; Total fat: 23g; Total carbs: 38g; Sugar: 4g; Protein: 36g; Fiber: 2g; Sodium: 983mg

Unstuffed Cabbage Roll Skillet

Cabbage rolls are another one of those dishes that are a true labor of love. This is fine if it's a Sunday afternoon and you have an hour or more to spare. But on a weeknight when you need dinner on the table stat, it's impossible. This recipe solves the time-constraint issue of weeknight cooking because the beef and rice mixture is cooked with the cabbage leaves, all in one skillet.

ONE POT

PREP TIME: 10 minutes
COOK TIME: 20 minutes
SERVES: 2

8 ounces lean ground beef, 10 percent fat

1 small onion, diced

2 garlic cloves, minced

½ small head green cabbage, chopped (about 4 cups)

½ cup rice

1 (14-ounce) can diced tomatoes

1 cup water

¼ teaspoon salt

2 tablespoons chopped fresh parsley

1. **Cook the beef and onion.** In a medium skillet over medium-high heat, cook the ground beef, onion, and garlic, breaking the beef into small pieces as it cooks to ensure it browns evenly and there is no pink left, 5 to 7 minutes.

2. **Cook the cabbage and rice.** Add the cabbage, rice, tomatoes, water, and salt, stirring well to combine. Bring to a boil, reduce heat, and cover. Simmer for 15 minutes, until the rice is cooked.

3. **Garnish.** Top with the fresh parsley. Serve and enjoy.

TIP: I like to use fire-roasted diced tomatoes with basil and garlic in this recipe. It adds even more flavor to the dish. To cut down on prep time, you can buy a bag of preshredded cabbage.

SWAP: To make this dish heartier, swap the rice for quinoa. You'll increase the protein content by doing that, as well.

Per serving: Calories: 390; Total fat: 9g; Total carbs: 48g; Sugar: 7g; Protein: 29g; Fiber: 4g; Sodium: 380mg

Italian Stuffed Pepper Skillet

Stuffed peppers are a delicious dinner option, but they require a long bake time. To cut down on that time, I chop up the peppers and put them into a skillet. The result is the flavor of stuffed peppers in a dish that's ready for the table in 30 minutes.

ONE POT

PREP TIME: 5 minutes
COOK TIME: 25 minutes
SERVES: 2

8 ounces lean ground beef, 10 percent fat

1 small green bell pepper, seeded and chopped

½ onion, diced

½ teaspoon salt, divided

2 teaspoons Italian seasoning, divided

⅓ cup white rice

1½ cups jarred marinara sauce

½ cup beef broth

1 cup shredded Italian cheese blend

1. **Cook the beef and vegetables.** In a medium skillet over medium-high heat, cook the beef, bell pepper, and onion. Break the beef up into small pieces as you go. Cook until the beef is browned and vegetables are soft, 7 to 8 minutes. Season with ¼ teaspoon of salt and 1 teaspoon of Italian seasoning.

2. **Cook the rice.** Add the rice, marinara sauce, beef broth, remaining 1 teaspoon of Italian seasoning, and remaining ¼ teaspoon of salt. Stir to combine. Bring to a boil, then reduce the heat and cover. Cook until the rice is tender, about 15 minutes, stirring occasionally.

3. **Top with the cheese.** Sprinkle the skillet with the Italian cheese blend and cover, letting the cheese melt for 1 to 2 minutes.

4. **Serve.** Spoon onto plates and enjoy.

TIP: Instant rice can help decrease the cooking time by up to 10 minutes, making this a super quick meal.

SWAP: The green bell pepper has a fairly strong flavor. For a subtler dish, opt for red bell pepper instead. Italian sausage also works well here instead of ground beef.

Per serving: Calories: 426; Total fat: 13g; Total carbs: 42g; Sugar: 13g; Protein: 34g; Fiber: 5g; Sodium: 1936mg

One-Skillet Shepherd's Pie

This recipe uses a cheat: premade refrigerated mashed potatoes. Once you taste it, you'll understand why I had to include it in this cookbook. Save this recipe for a cold winter night when you crave warm comfort food.

ONE POT

PREP TIME: 10 minutes
COOK TIME: 15 minutes
SERVES: 2 or 3

1 tablespoon extra-virgin olive oil

4 ounces lean ground beef, 10 percent fat

½ small white onion, chopped

¼ teaspoon salt

2 cups frozen mixed vegetables (corn, peas, carrots, and green beans)

2 tablespoons flour

1 tablespoon Worcestershire sauce

½ cup beef broth

12 ounces refrigerated mashed potatoes

1. **Cook the beef and onion.** In an 8- or 9-inch cast-iron skillet over medium-high heat, heat the olive oil. Add the beef, onion, and salt. Cook until the beef is browned and cooked through and the onion is softened, 5 to 7 minutes. Add the mixed vegetables and stir to combine.

2. **Preheat the broiler.** While the beef and onion are cooking, preheat the broiler to high.

3. **Thicken the mixture.** In the same skillet, add the flour and stir, cooking for 1 minute. Add the Worcestershire sauce and beef broth. Stir to combine and cook for 2 more minutes until the mixture slightly thickens.

4. **Top with the mashed potatoes.** Spread the mashed potatoes on top of the beef mixture.

5. **Broil the pie.** Place the cast-iron skillet in the oven and broil for 2 to 3 minutes, until the top is evenly browned.

6. **Serve.** Scoop the pie onto two plates and enjoy.

TIP: Most refrigerated mashed potatoes come in a 24-ounce package, so you can use the leftover mashed potatoes from this meal to accompany Pan-Seared Steaks with Gorgonzola Sauce (page 124).

SWAP: Use mashed cauliflower instead of mashed potatoes. You can find it in the vegetable section of the freezer aisle.

Per serving: Calories: 398; Total fat: 14g; Total carbs: 49g; Sugar: 5g; Protein: 20g; Fiber: 5g; Sodium: 1018mg

Chimichurri Grilled Steak

Chimichurri is a universal sauce that can be used in so many different dishes, but pairing it with grilled steak is by far my favorite. I like throwing a bunch of vegetables on the grill with the steaks to round out this dinner. Don't forget to drizzle some of the chimichurri on the veggies, too.

SUPER QUICK

PREP TIME: 10 minutes
COOK TIME: 10 minutes
SERVES: 2

¼ cup chopped
fresh parsley

2 tablespoons chopped
fresh cilantro

3 tablespoons
extra-virgin olive oil

1 garlic clove

1 shallot, minced

1 tablespoon red
wine vinegar

⅛ teaspoon salt,
plus pinch

1 (1-pound) sirloin steak

Pinch freshly ground
black pepper

1. **Make the chimichurri.** In a food processor, combine the parsley, cilantro, oil, garlic, shallot, vinegar, and ⅛ teaspoon of salt, and pulse until combined.

2. **Prep the steak.** Pat the steaks dry and season with a pinch salt and pepper.

3. **Preheat the grill to high heat.**

4. **Cook the steak.** Grill the steak for 3 to 5 minutes on each side, or until the meat is cooked to your liking.

5. **Top it off.** Top the steaks with chimichurri. Serve and enjoy.

TIP: Be sure to get your grill hot. Cooking the steaks over high heat gives them gorgeous grill marks and seals in the juices. For medium-rare steaks, cook 2 to 3 minutes on each side, depending on the thickness of your steak. For medium steaks, cook 3 to 5 minutes, and for medium-well, 5 to 7 minutes on each side.

SWAP: Traditional chimichurri calls for parsley and cilantro, but sometimes I use different herbs, such as basil or rosemary, for a fresh take on a classic sauce.

Per serving: Calories: 491; Total fat: 30g; Total carbs: 2g; Sugar: 0g; Protein: 52g; Fiber: 0g; Sodium: 145mg

Pan-Seared Steaks with Gorgonzola Sauce

When my husband and I crave steak, but don't want to pay the big bucks at a restaurant, we always make this dish. The key is cooking pan-seared steak in a wicked-hot cast-iron skillet. Preheating the pan will give the steaks a delicious crust. Fair warning: The Gorgonzola sauce may cause you to lick your plate clean.

PREP TIME: 5 minutes
COOK TIME: 20 minutes
SERVES: 2

2 tablespoons butter, divided

2 (6-ounce) sirloin steaks

Salt

Freshly ground black pepper

1 small shallot, diced

1 garlic clove, minced

1 tablespoon flour

¼ cup heavy cream

¼ cup crumbled Gorgonzola cheese

1. **Prepare.** Preheat a cast-iron skillet over high heat for 5 minutes, until the pan is hot. Melt 1 tablespoon of butter in the skillet.

2. **Cook the steaks.** Season the steaks with salt and pepper, and add them to the pan. Cook to your preferred doneness. For medium-rare, this is 2 to 3 minutes on each side, depending on the thickness of your steak. For medium, cook for 3 to 5 minutes on each side, and for medium-well, cook for 5 to 7 minutes on each side. Let the steaks rest for 5 minutes.

3. **Make the Gorgonzola cream sauce.** While the steaks are cooking, make the cream sauce. In a small saucepan over medium heat, melt the remaining 1 tablespoon of butter. Add the shallot and garlic, and cook until softened, about 3 minutes. Stir in the flour, and cook for

1 minute. Add the cream and bring to a simmer. Stir in the Gorgonzola cheese until it melts. Season with salt and pepper.

4. **Top it off.** Top the steaks with the sauce. Serve and enjoy.

TIP: This recipe is tailor-made for the outdoor grill. You can cook the steaks straight on the grill or in your cast-iron skillet over the grill.

SWAP: Sirloin steaks are an excellent, inexpensive choice, but if you want to splurge, go for a rib eye or New York strip steak.

Per serving: Calories: 521; Total fat: 35g; Total carbs: 6g; Sugar: 0g; Protein: 44g; Fiber: 1g; Sodium: 438mg

Whipped Ricotta with Grilled Peaches, *page 131*

CHAPTER EIGHT

DESSERT

Desserts are often the most challenging dishes to prepare for two people. Most recipes are scaled to yield anywhere from 8 to 24 servings. I've changed all of that here. In this chapter you will find a combination of cookies, brownies, mini cakes, and even cheesecake cups that make just enough for two people. Your sweet tooth will be satisfied, but you won't have the extra servings around that you feel obligated to eat.

Peanut Butter Cup Shakes

When my husband and I go out for ice cream, we have completely different preferences. I like my ice cream filled with all the chunks—brownie bites, swirls of peanut butter, cookies pieces, you name it. My husband is more of a purist, and likes his ice cream simple and smooth. When we're at home, I make these Peanut Butter Cup Shakes to please us both. I get some texture from the puréed peanut butter cups, but it's still relatively smooth. I even top mine with a couple more chopped peanut butter cups for extra chunks.

5-INGREDIENT
SUPER QUICK
VEGETARIAN

PREP TIME: 5 minutes
SERVES: 2

3 cups chocolate ice cream

⅔ cup milk

3 tablespoons creamy peanut butter

8 mini peanut butter cups, plus 4 additional mini peanut butter cups, chopped

1. **Blend.** In a blender, put the ice cream, milk, and peanut butter and blend on high speed until combined.

2. **Add the peanut butter cups.** Add the peanut butter cups to the blender and pulse until blended.

3. **Serve.** Divide between two glasses and top with the chopped peanut butter cups. Serve and enjoy.

SWAP: The chocolate ice cream and peanut butter cups can make for a very rich treat. Vanilla is a good option to keep the flavors on the lighter side. Oreos also work well here.

Per serving: Calories: 574; Total fat: 35g; Total carbs: 55g; Sugar: 47g; Protein: 16g; Fiber: 4g; Sodium: 322mg

Chocolate–Peanut Butter Banana Splits

I love an old-fashioned banana split. But I have to say, I might love these even more. I replace the crushed pineapple and strawberries found in a traditional banana split with peanuts, peanut butter, and peanut butter cups. As far as I'm concerned, this combination can do no wrong! I don't take out the cherry or whipped cream, though—those are non-negotiable.

SUPER QUICK
VEGETARIAN

PREP TIME: 10 minutes
SERVES: 2

¼ cup jarred hot
fudge sauce

2 tablespoons creamy
peanut butter

2 bananas, halved
lengthwise

4 scoops vanilla
ice cream

2 tablespoons
peanuts, chopped

¼ cup chopped peanut
butter cups

Whipped cream

2 maraschino cherries

1. **Prepare.** Warm the hot fudge sauce according to the jar instructions. Place the peanut butter in a small microwave-safe bowl, and microwave for 15 seconds, until warm.

2. **Assemble.** Place the banana halves in two bowls. Top each with 2 scoops of ice cream, hot fudge sauce, warm peanut butter, chopped peanuts, and peanut butter cups.

3. **Top it off.** Top each with some whipped cream and a cherry. Serve and enjoy.

SWAP: You can swap the peanuts, peanut butter, and peanut butter cups for almonds, almond butter, and almond butter cups, or for chocolate-covered almonds.

Per serving: Calories: 819; Total fat: 47g; Total carbs: 95g; Sugar: 65g; Protein: 14g; Fiber: 6g; Sodium: 272mg

Whipped Ricotta with Grilled Peaches

Even with desserts, sometimes the simplest ingredient goes a long way. Just 5 minutes on the grill transforms peaches from a snack to an irresistible dessert. The ricotta cheese feels sophisticated, but it's really quite simple. If you're feeling really fancy, you can top this dish off with a sprig of mint.

5-INGREDIENT
SUPER QUICK
VEGETARIAN

PREP TIME: 15 minutes
COOK TIME: 5 minutes
SERVES: 2

½ cup whole-milk ricotta cheese

2 tablespoons heavy cream

2 tablespoons honey, divided

1 teaspoon pure vanilla extract

2 peaches, halved and pitted

1. **Prepare.** Preheat the grill to medium heat.

2. **Make the whipped ricotta cheese.** In a small bowl, whip together the ricotta cheese, heavy cream, 1 tablespoon of honey, and the vanilla.

3. **Grill the peaches.** Brush the flesh side of the peaches with the remaining 1 tablespoon of honey. Grill the peaches flesh-side down for 4 to 5 minutes, until you see grill marks.

4. **Serve.** Top the peaches with a dollop of the whipped ricotta cheese. Serve and enjoy.

TIP: If you have leftover ricotta cheese in your container, save it for Skillet Lasagna (page 118).

SWAP: Any kind of stone fruit will work in this recipe, including nectarines, plums, and apricots.

Per serving: Calories: 235; Total fat: 10g; Total carbs: 33g; Sugar: 31g; Protein: 5g; Fiber: 2g; Sodium: 33mg

White Chocolate–Cranberry Oatmeal Cookies

Oatmeal cookies can run anywhere from thin and crispy to really thick and chewy. My preference falls somewhere in the middle. These oatmeal cookies are just how I like them—crispy on the outside and chewy on the inside. This recipe makes six cookies: the perfect amount to share between two people with a couple for the next day.

SUPER QUICK
VEGETARIAN

PREP TIME: 10 minutes
COOK TIME: 10 minutes
SERVES: 2

2 tablespoons unsalted butter, at room temperature

1 tablespoon granulated sugar

3 tablespoons brown sugar

¼ teaspoon pure vanilla extract

1 egg yolk

¼ cup all-purpose flour

⅓ cup old-fashioned oats

¼ teaspoon baking soda

¼ teaspoon salt

2 tablespoons dried cranberries

2 tablespoons white chocolate chips

1. **Prepare.** Preheat the oven to 350°F. Line a baking sheet with parchment paper.

2. **Combine the wet ingredients.** In a medium bowl, beat the butter, granulated sugar, and brown sugar until creamy. Add the vanilla and the egg yolk, beating until combined.

3. **Mix the dry ingredients.** In a small bowl, stir together the flour, oats, baking soda, and salt. Add the flour mixture to the butter and sugar mixture, beating until combined.

4. **Add the remaining ingredients.** Fold in the cranberries and the white chocolate chips.

5. **Make the cookies.** Form the dough into 6 cookies and place on the prepared baking sheet.

6. **Bake.** Bake for 8 to 10 minutes, until the edges are golden. Serve and enjoy.

SWAP: For an extra-decadent oatmeal cookie, use semi-sweet chocolate chips instead of white chocolate chips, and pecans instead of cranberries.

Per serving: Calories: 388; Total fat: 18g; Total carbs: 54g; Sugar: 35g; Protein: 5g; Fiber: 2g; Sodium: 551mg

Salted Caramel–Chocolate Chip Cookies

I first stumbled upon the flavor of salted caramel at an ice cream shop in Seattle about seven years ago. To this day, it's still one of my favorite flavors. I'm a sucker for pretty much anything with salted caramel—I love the combination of salty and sweet.

VEGETARIAN

PREP TIME: 15 minutes
COOK TIME: 10 minutes
SERVES: 2 or 3

3 tablespoons unsalted butter

¼ cup light brown sugar

2 tablespoons granulated sugar

½ teaspoon pure vanilla extract

1 large egg yolk

½ cup all-purpose flour

½ teaspoon baking soda

2 tablespoons semisweet chocolate chips

2 tablespoons caramel chips

Sea salt

1. **Prepare.** Preheat the oven to 325°F. Line a baking sheet with parchment paper.

2. **Warm the butter.** Using a microwave-safe bowl, microwave the butter on high for 20 seconds. The butter should be soft, but not completely melted.

3. **Add the sugar.** Whisk in the brown sugar and granulated sugar until well combined.

4. **Add the vanilla and egg yolk.** Whisk in the vanilla and egg yolk until well combined.

5. **Add the dry ingredients.** Stir in the flour and baking soda.

6. **Add the chocolate and caramel chips.** Fold the chocolate and caramel chips into the dough.

7. **Form into dough balls.** Roll the dough into balls that are equal in size to about 2 tablespoons, and place them on the prepared baking sheet. Sprinkle with sea salt. You should have about 8 cookies.

8. **Bake.** Bake in the preheated oven for 9 to 11 minutes, until the edges are golden brown. Do not overbake these—you want them to be slightly undercooked in the middle so they stay chewy. Serve and enjoy.

Per serving: Calories: 570; Total fat: 30g; Total carbs: 73g; Sugar: 47g; Protein: 7g; Fiber: 1g; Sodium: 599mg

Peanut Butter–Chocolate Chip Cookie Dough Bites

Confession: When I make cookies, I'm in it just for the cookie dough about half the time. Sure, I'll have a couple of baked cookies, but I'm just as happy eating a spoonful or two of the dough. Since eating raw eggs can make you sick, though, I came up with this recipe for eggless peanut butter cookie dough bites. I also scaled it down because I really don't need to eat an entire batch of raw cookie dough. You should roll these into dough bites, but I won't judge if you eat them straight from the bowl with a spoon!

SUPER QUICK
VEGETARIAN

PREP TIME: 15 minutes
SERVES: 2 or 3

2 tablespoons unsalted butter, at room temperature

2 tablespoons creamy peanut butter

2 tablespoons granulated sugar

1 tablespoon brown sugar

1½ tablespoons milk

¼ teaspoon pure vanilla extract

½ cup all-purpose flour

¼ teaspoon salt

¼ cup mini chocolate chips

1. **Beat the butter and sugar.** In a small bowl, mix the butter, peanut butter, granulated sugar, and brown sugar with an electric mixer, until light and fluffy, about 3 minutes.

2. **Add the remaining ingredients.** Add the milk, vanilla, flour, and salt, and beat until combined. Stir in the chocolate chips.

3. **Roll into bites.** Using a tablespoon, portion out the dough and shape into balls. Serve and enjoy.

TIP: You can make these without an electric mixer by just beating the ingredients together with a fork. (The texture is a little lighter if you use an electric mixer, but it's not necessary.) These can be stored in the refrigerator for 2 to 3 days in an airtight container.

SWAP: Depending on the type of chocolate you prefer, you can use semisweet chocolate chips, dark chocolate chips, or milk chocolate chips.

Per serving: Calories: 541; Total fat: 28g; Total carbs: 64g; Sugar: 35g; Protein: 10g; Fiber: 2g; Sodium: 455mg

Avocado Chocolate Mousse

Yes, you read that correctly: Avocado Chocolate Mousse. I promise it won't taste like you're eating chocolate guacamole. This mousse is rich and creamy, and intensely chocolatey. You can add a dollop of whipped cream to balance out the deep chocolate flavor.

5-INGREDIENT
SUPER QUICK
VEGETARIAN

PREP TIME: 10 minutes
SERVES: 2

½ cup semisweet chocolate chips

2 tablespoons unsweetened cocoa powder

2 tablespoons milk

1 large ripe avocado, peeled and pitted

½ teaspoon pure vanilla extract

Pinch sea salt

1. **Melt the chocolate.** In a small microwave-safe bowl, add the chocolate chips. Microwave in 30-second increments, stirring between each one, until melted.

2. **Combine the ingredients.** In a small food processor, put the melted chocolate, cocoa powder, milk, avocado, vanilla, and salt. Pulse until smooth.

3. **Serve.** Divide the mousse evenly between two bowls. Serve and enjoy.

TIP: When choosing an avocado, you want to find one that is slightly softened but not overly so. If you pick the stem off, it should be green, not brown, underneath.

SWAP: Don't have a ripe avocado? You can use 6 ounces of silken tofu instead. Follow the instructions as written previously. The silken tofu will easily purée in a food processor.

Per serving: Calories: 185; Total fat: 16g; Total carbs: 14g; Sugar: 3g; Protein: 4g; Fiber: 8g; Sodium: 132mg

Caramel-Stuffed Brownie Bites

Sometimes when I'm craving chocolate, a classic brownie will do. But other times, I want a little something extra. It's times like these that I dig into my caramel stash and make these decadent bites. The small batch here is key since it allows me to indulge, but doesn't leave me with a ton of leftovers.

VEGETARIAN

PREP TIME: 10 minutes
COOK TIME: 20 minutes
SERVES: 2

Nonstick cooking spray

5 tablespoons
unsalted butter

⅓ cup plus
2 tablespoons
granulated sugar

¼ cup unsweetened
cocoa powder

¼ teaspoon salt

½ teaspoon
vanilla extract

1 large egg

¼ cup all-purpose flour

6 soft caramels

1. **Prepare.** Preheat the oven to 350°F. Lightly coat six cavities of a mini muffin pan with nonstick cooking spray.

2. **Melt the butter.** In a microwave-safe bowl, microwave the butter for 30 seconds. It does not need to be completely melted, just very soft.

3. **Combine the ingredients.** In the same bowl, add the granulated sugar, cocoa powder, salt, vanilla, egg, and flour, mixing well to combine.

4. **Assemble.** Spoon the brownie batter into the prepared muffin cups, filling them about halfway. Place the caramels on top of the batter and then top each caramel with more batter.

5. **Bake.** Bake in the preheated oven for 15 to 17 minutes.

6. **Let cool.** Let the brownies cool on a baking rack for 3 minutes, then remove from the muffin pan. Serve and enjoy.

TIP: If you're a fan of salted caramel, be sure to sprinkle some sea salt on top of these before putting them in the oven.

SWAP: For a truly decadent dessert, try miniature peanut butter cups instead of caramel.

Per serving: Calories: 678; Total fat: 35g; Total carbs: 91g; Sugar: 70g; Protein: 9g; Fiber: 4g; Sodium: 607mg

Raspberry Oat Cups

These oat cups could also be considered a breakfast dish, but since I try not to eat refined sugar at breakfast, this is a dessert recipe in my house. Whatever you consider this recipe to be, I'm sure you'll find it delicious. It's like a mini raspberry pie, but with a healthier crust.

VEGETARIAN

PREP TIME: 10 minutes
COOK TIME: 20 minutes
SERVES: 2 or 3

Nonstick cooking spray

¼ cup unsalted butter

3 tablespoons granulated sugar

2 tablespoons brown sugar

½ teaspoon pure vanilla extract

½ cup all-purpose flour

⅓ cup old-fashioned oats

Pinch salt

¼ cup raspberry jam

1. **Prepare.** Preheat the oven to 375°F. Lightly coat four cavities of a muffin pan with nonstick cooking spray.

2. **Make the dough.** In a medium microwave-safe bowl, melt the butter in the microwave. Add the granulated sugar, brown sugar, and vanilla, and stir well to combine. Add the flour, oats, and salt, and stir well to combine. Remove ¼ cup of the mixture and set aside.

3. **Assemble.** Press 2 tablespoons of the dough into the bottom of each prepared muffin cup. Spoon 1 tablespoon of the jam over each, and then spread the remaining dough over the jam, about 1 tablespoon per oat cup.

4. **Bake.** Bake in the preheated oven for 15 to 20 minutes, until lightly golden brown.

5. **Cool.** Let the oat cups cool slightly, then remove them from the muffin pan.

6. **Serve.** Serve topped with ice cream, whipped cream, or yogurt, and enjoy.

TIP: Leftovers can make a great breakfast crumbled into a bowl of yogurt.

SWAP: While I prefer raspberry jam in this recipe, any other kind of jam will work here, particularly apricot or strawberry.

Per serving: Calories: 547; Total fat: 24g; Total carbs: 81g; Sugar: 45g; Protein: 5g; Fiber: 2g; Sodium: 245mg

Mini Strawberry Crisps

There's something about mini desserts that are more appealing than regular sized ones. Maybe it's that we feel like we are being less indulgent, or maybe it's just because miniature sized anything is cute. Regardless, I love making fruit crisps in ramekins because it's just plain fun! I pretty much always top my strawberry crisp with a scoop or two of vanilla ice cream. If the weather is pleasant, they are even more delicious enjoyed outside on the patio.

VEGETARIAN

PREP TIME: 10 minutes
COOK TIME: 20 minutes
SERVES: 2

2½ cups finely diced fresh strawberries

1 tablespoon granulated sugar

3 tablespoons brown sugar, divided

½ teaspoon pure vanilla extract

4 tablespoons flour, divided

3 tablespoons oats

¼ teaspoon salt

2 tablespoons butter

1. **Prepare.** Preheat the oven to 400°F.

2. **Make the strawberry filling.** In a medium bowl, mix the strawberries, granulated sugar, 1 tablespoon of brown sugar, the vanilla, and 2 tablespoons of flour.

3. **Fill the ramekins.** Evenly distribute the strawberry mixture between two 8-ounce glass ramekins.

4. **Make the crisp topping.** In a small bowl, mix the remaining 2 tablespoons of brown sugar, the remaining 2 tablespoons of flour, and the oats, salt, and butter.

5. **Assemble.** Sprinkle the crisp topping over the strawberries.

6. **Bake.** Bake in the preheated oven for 20 minutes.

7. **Cool.** Cool for 1 to 2 minutes. Serve and enjoy.

TIP: These are best served topped with vanilla ice cream or whipped cream.

SWAP: For a dairy-free version, use coconut oil instead of butter in the crisp topping, and serve it with dairy-free ice cream.

Per serving: Calories: 331; Total fat: 13g; Total carbs: 53g; Sugar: 30g; Protein: 4g; Fiber: 5g; Sodium: 379mg

No-Bake Strawberry Cheesecake Cups

I first made this recipe on a larger scale for a Valentine's Day party that we host every year. The pink color of these strawberry cheesecake cups is festive, and they are light enough to enjoy after a big meal. They're also a great date-night-in dessert!

SUPER QUICK
VEGETARIAN

PREP TIME: 15 minutes
SERVES: 2

½ cup fresh
strawberries, diced

⅓ cup heavy
whipping cream

4 ounces cream cheese,
at room temperature

¼ cup powdered sugar

½ teaspoon
vanilla extract

¼ cup graham cracker
crumbs, plus more
for serving

1. **Purée the strawberries.** In a blender or food processor, place the strawberries and blend until very few chunks remain.

2. **Beat the heavy cream.** In a medium bowl, mix the heavy whipping cream with an electric mixer until stiff peaks form, about 2 minutes. Set aside.

3. **Beat the cream cheese.** In another medium bowl, beat the cream cheese, powdered sugar, and vanilla using an electric mixer until the mixture becomes fluffy, about 2 minutes. Add the strawberry purée, and beat using the mixer until combined.

4. **Fold in the whipped cream.** Gently fold the whipped cream into the strawberry cream cheese mixture.

5. **Assemble.** Coat the bottom of two bowls or cups with the graham cracker crumbs. Top with the strawberry cheesecake mixture.

6. **Top it off.** Top with additional graham cracker crumbs. Serve and enjoy.

TIP: To save yourself a little bit of prep time, use store-bought whipped cream instead of making it from scratch.

SWAP: For a more decadent chocolate and strawberry combination, use chocolate cookie crumbs as the base for this recipe.

Per serving: Calories: 454; Total fat: 36g; Total carbs: 29g; Sugar: 19g; Protein: 6g; Fiber: 1g; Sodium: 277mg

Confetti Cake Shortbread

Adding sprinkles to desserts automatically makes them more fun, right? This short-bread recipe has been adapted to cook in a loaf pan with the delightful addition of added sprinkles. It's made even more delicious topped with ice cream or dipped in chocolate.

5-INGREDIENT
VEGETARIAN

PREP TIME: 5 minutes
COOK TIME: 25 minutes
SERVES: 2 or 3

Nonstick cooking spray

½ cup unsalted butter, at room temperature

⅓ cup sugar

1 teaspoon pure vanilla extract

¼ teaspoon salt

1 cup all-purpose unbleached flour

¼ cup sprinkles

1. **Prepare.** Preheat the oven to 350°F. Line a loaf pan with parchment paper and spray with nonstick cooking spray.

2. **Beat the butter and sugar.** In a small bowl, mix the butter and sugar using an electric mixer for about 1 minute, or until combined.

3. **Add the remaining ingredients.** Add the vanilla, salt, and flour, stirring to combine. Stir in the sprinkles.

4. **Bake the shortbread.** Pour the dough into the bottom of the prepared pan. Bake for 20 to 25 minutes, until lightly golden on the edges.

5. **Serve.** Cut into four slices. Serve and enjoy.

TIP: I like to use a mini loaf pan when baking cakes for just two people. That way there aren't a ton of leftovers. Plus, the smaller pan speeds up the baking time!

SWAP: For an almond-orange shortbread variation, use almond extract instead of vanilla extract and zest from half of an orange instead of sprinkles.

Per serving: Calories: 713; Total fat: 52g; Total carbs: 64g; Sugar: 52g; Protein: 3g; Fiber: 0g; Sodium: 297mg

Mini Churro Bites

Refrigerated biscuit dough, cinnamon, and sugar combine to create this super tasty dessert! I am not a huge fan of frying things, but these require a little bit of oil to get them to golden-brown perfection. Serve with warm caramel sauce for an extra dose of decadence.

5-INGREDIENT
VEGETARIAN

PREP TIME: 10 minutes
COOK TIME: 15 minutes
SERVES: 2 or 3

1 cup vegetable oil

1 (6-ounce) container refrigerated biscuits

¼ cup sugar

1 teaspoon cinnamon

½ cup caramel sauce

1. **Heat the oil.** In a small saucepan over medium-high heat, add the oil and heat. There should be about 1 inch of oil on the bottom of the pan.

2. **Prepare the biscuit dough.** Cut the biscuit dough into 1-inch pieces.

3. **Make the cinnamon sugar.** In a small bowl, combine the sugar and cinnamon.

4. **Cook the churros.** Drop 4 or 5 biscuit pieces into the hot oil and cook for 30 to 45 seconds. With a slotted spoon, flip and cook them for another 30 seconds, until they're golden brown. Immediately remove them from the pan of oil, and place on a paper towel–lined plate.

5. **Roll in the cinnamon sugar.** Once cool enough to touch, roll the fried dough in the cinnamon sugar. Repeat with the remaining pieces.

6. **Warm the caramel sauce.** Microwave the caramel sauce in a small microwave-safe bowl, until warm.

7. **Dip.** Dip the mini churro bites in warmed-up caramel sauce. Serve and enjoy.

TIP: These can also be baked. Preheat the oven to 350°F. Place the churro bites on a baking sheet and bake for 12 to 13 minutes. Then continue with the recipe.

SWAP: Try dipping the churros in hot fudge sauce instead of caramel sauce, or serve the churros with both.

Per serving: Calories: 734; Total fat: 25g; Total carbs: 122g; Sugar: 79g; Protein: 6g; Fiber: 1g; Sodium: 920mg

Caramel-Apple Hand Pies

I've never been much of a pie baker because the thought of a homemade piecrust intimidates me. Plus, making an entire pie for just me and my husband seems excessive. Mini pies, on the other hand, are just right. A small can of refrigerated crescent rolls gives these hand pies a soft and flaky outer layer. The pies are best served warm, straight from the oven, and topped with a scoop of vanilla ice cream.

VEGETARIAN

PREP TIME: 10 minutes
COOK TIME: 20 minutes
SERVES: 2

1 tablespoon butter

1 Granny Smith apple, peeled, cored, and sliced

2 tablespoons brown sugar

½ teaspoon cinnamon

⅛ teaspoon nutmeg

1 (4-ounce) can refrigerated crescent rolls

2 tablespoons caramel sauce

Vanilla ice cream

1. **Prepare.** Preheat the oven to 400°F. Line a baking sheet with parchment paper.

2. **Sauté the apples.** In a medium skillet over medium-high heat, heat the butter. Add the apple slices, brown sugar, cinnamon, and nutmeg. Cook until the apples are soft, about 5 minutes.

3. **Prepare the crescent roll dough.** Roll out the crescent roll dough and separate into triangles. Place a couple of apple slices at the wide end of each triangle and gently roll up.

4. **Bake.** Place the hand pies on the prepared baking sheet. Bake in the preheated oven for 11 to 12 minutes, until golden brown. Place on a baking rack to cool.

5. **Warm the caramel sauce.** While the hand pies are baking, microwave the caramel sauce in a small microwave-safe bowl, until warm. Drizzle the sauce over the baked hand pies.

6. **Top it off.** Top with a scoop of vanilla ice cream, and serve.

SWAP: For a change in flavor, try pears in this recipe. The cooking time won't change much, and pears and caramel complement each other nicely.

Per serving: Calories: 417; Total fat: 18g; Total carbs: 60g; Sugar: 24g; Protein: 5g; Fiber: 3g; Sodium: 556mg

Molten Chocolate Lava Cakes

When I have to choose between vanilla and chocolate, I will always, without a doubt, choose chocolate. These lava cakes are perfect for when that chocolate craving strikes and a handful of chocolate chips just isn't enough. I prefer to top these cakes with ice cream, but salted caramel and powdered sugar are also great options.

VEGETARIAN

PREP TIME: 10 minutes
COOK TIME: 15 minutes
SERVES: 2

Nonstick cooking spray

4 tablespoons
unsalted butter

½ cup semisweet
chocolate chips

½ cup powdered sugar

¼ teaspoon salt

1 large egg

½ teaspoon pure
vanilla extract

¼ cup unbleached
all-purpose flour

Ice cream, salted
caramel, or powdered
sugar, optional

1. **Prepare.** Preheat the oven to 425°F. Lightly coat two ramekins with nonstick cooking spray.

2. **Melt the butter and chocolate.** In a microwave-safe bowl, combine the butter and chocolate chips. Microwave in 20-second increments, stirring well between each session. Repeat until melted, about 1 minute.

3. **Stir in the remaining ingredients.** Add the powdered sugar and salt, and whisk well. Add the egg and vanilla, whisking again. Stir in the flour, mixing until just combined. Divide the batter between the ramekins.

4. **Bake.** Bake for 10 to 12 minutes, until the cake is puffed but the center isn't set.

5. **Serve.** Top with ice cream, salted caramel, or powdered sugar, if desired, and serve.

TIP: Many recipes for molten cake call for chopped chocolate, but I think chocolate chips work just as well. Plus, using chips saves time because you don't have to do any chopping.

SWAP: If you want to turn up the decadence, swap in dark chocolate chips. They have more cacao and add an even deeper, richer flavor to this dessert.

Per serving: Calories: 230; Total fat: 4g; Total carbs: 45g; Sugar: 32g; Protein: 5g; Fiber: 1g; Sodium: 326mg

MEASUREMENT AND CONVERSION TABLES

OVEN TEMPERATURES

FAHRENHEIT	CELSIUS (APPROXIMATE)
250°F	120°C
300°F	150°C
325°F	165°C
350°F	180°C
375°F	190°C
400°F	200°C
425°F	220°C
450°F	230°C

VOLUME EQUIVALENTS (LIQUID)

U.S. STANDARD	U.S. STANDARD (OUNCES)	METRIC (APPROXIMATE)
2 tablespoons	1 fl. oz.	30 mL
¼ cup	2 fl. oz.	60 mL
½ cup	4 fl. oz.	120 mL
1 cup	8 fl. oz.	240 mL
1½ cups	12 fl. oz.	355 mL
2 cups or 1 pint	16 fl. oz.	475 mL
4 cups or 1 quart	32 fl. oz.	1 L
1 gallon	128 fl. oz.	4 L

WEIGHT EQUIVALENTS

U.S. STANDARD	METRIC (APPROXIMATE)
½ ounce	15 g
1 ounce	30 g
2 ounces	60 g
4 ounces	115 g
8 ounces	225 g
12 ounces	340 g
16 ounces or 1 pound	455 g

VOLUME EQUIVALENTS (DRY)

U.S. STANDARD	METRIC (APPROXIMATE)
⅛ teaspoon	0.5 mL
¼ teaspoon	1 mL
½ teaspoon	2 mL
¾ teaspoon	4 mL
1 teaspoon	5 mL
1 tablespoon	15 mL
¼ cup	59 mL
⅓ cup	79 mL
½ cup	118 mL
⅔ cup	156 mL
¾ cup	177 mL
1 cup	235 mL
2 cups or 1 pint	475 mL
3 cups	700 mL
4 cups or 1 quart	1 L

RECIPE INDEX

INDEX

ACKNOWLEDGMENTS

First and foremost, this cookbook would not have been possible without the support of my husband. He's my number one fan and most trusted taste tester. My other number one fans are my parents. They've always encouraged me to dream big and to believe in the power of hard work. A big thanks to my other supporters and recipe testers, including my in-laws, Aunt Penny, Jordan, Paige, Olivia, Megan, Sonja, the St. Olaf crew, and all of my blog readers!

ABOUT THE AUTHOR

 **Taylor Ellingson** is a self-taught baker and home cook who loves creating healthy meals and decadent desserts. Even more, she loves introducing people to cooking and showing them how accessible and easy it can be. She is the founder of the food blog *greens & chocolate* (www.greensnchocolate.com), where she blogs mostly about her recipe creations and occasionally about her family and their travel adventures. When she's not cooking and eating, she enjoys running, yoga, hiking, travel, patio happy hours, and spending time with her family. She was born and raised in Iowa and currently lives in Minneapolis, Minnesota, with her husband, Marc, and their two boys, Lars and Soren.

CPSIA information can be obtained
at www.ICGtesting.com
Printed in the USA
BVHW05s0043101018
529702BV00001B/1/P